1961

Staughton Lynd
Anti-Federalism in Dutchess County,
New York

1962

Herbert Alan Johnson
The Law Merchant and Negotiable Instruments
in Colonial New York 1664 to 1730

Midwestern Books Competition 1963
American Institute of Graphic Arts Fifty Books of the Year 1964
Society of Typographic Arts 1964

1963

Charles H. Harris, III
The Sánchez Navarros: a Socio-economic
Study of a Coahuilan Latifundio 1846-1853

Midwestern Books Competition 1964

1964

No publishable manuscript submitted.

1965

David Paul Thelen
The Early Life of
Robert M. La Follette 1855-1884

WILLIAM P. LYONS MASTER'S ESSAY AWARD 1966

JACK D. ELLIS

*The French Socialists
and the
Problem of the Peace
1904-1914*

Et nous, nous disons aujourd'hui que l'affirmation de la paix est le plus grands des combats.

Jean Jaurès, *Discours pronouncé aux obséques de Francis de Pressensé,* January 1914

If we all were judged according to the consequences
Of all our words and deeds, beyond the intention
And beyond our limited understanding
Of ourselves and others, we should all be condemned.

T. S. Eliot, *The Cocktail Party*

JACK D. ELLIS

The French Socialists
and the
Problem of the Peace
1904-1914

LOYOLA UNIVERSITY PRESS

Chicago, Illinois

1967

About this book

The French Socialists and the Problem of the Peace 1904-1914 was designed by William Nicoll of Edit, Inc. It was set in the composing room of Loyola University Press. The text is 12/14 Bodoni Book; the reduced matter, 10/12; the notes, 8/10. The display type is 12 Bodoni Book caps.

It was printed by Photopress, Inc., on Warren's 60-pound English Finish paper and bound by A. C. Engdahl and Company, Inc., in Bancroft cloth.

PREFACE

I wish to acknowledge my debt to the following people who aided in the writing of this thesis: Professor Hans A. Schmitt, of Tulane University, who first stimulated my interest in pre-1914 French socialism by suggesting an examination of the French socialist role in the Dreyfus Affair of 1898, and whose constant enthusiasm and broad knowledge of early twentieth-century France greatly facilitated the task of writing; Professor John L. Snell, now of the University of Pennsylvania, who first encouraged me to analyze French socialist foreign policy views before the First World War, and in whose seminar in the spring of 1964 I completed my investigation for the critical years 1904-6; and Professors Francis G. James and Walter Sablinsky, both of Tulane, and William R. Savage, of Louisiana State University in New Orleans, who read the manuscript and offered invaluable suggestions.

In addition, I express my deepest appreciation to Mrs. Dorothy Whittemore, Reference Librarian of Tulane University Library, and to Miss Kathleen Blow, Chief Reference Librarian of the University of Texas, who gave generously of their time during the course of my research.

Finally, I wish to mention Professor Ralph L. Lynn, of Baylor University, a great and wise teacher who first stirred my interest in the past and who taught me that the study of history should, if nothing else, at least turn our attention and sympathies to men of the past who tried to better their own and our world.

JACK D. ELLIS

Tulane University

CONTENTS

I

_____

INTRODUCTION

The foreign policy of the French socialist party before the First World War has received only superficial treatment in the limited historiography of socialism under the Third Republic. This is particularly unfortunate in that the foreign policy concepts of the party, which were an important source of the bitter ideological duel that split the socialists and communists at Tours in 1920 and which played such a vital role in the Popular Front government of the 1930's, assumed many of their most characteristic features in the pre-1914 period, especially in regard to patriotism, pacifism, and internationalism. In 1953 Milorad M. Drachkovitch published the most comprehensive treatment to date of French socialist foreign policy attitudes before the tragedy of 1914,[1] but his volume deals primarily with the pacifist thought of Jean Jaurès and the debates on militarism and war at the party congresses.

The same is true of the numerous biographies of Jaurès,[2] the deputy for the Tarn and the most eloquent figure in the history of French socialism. Harold R. Weinstein, Marcelle Auclair, and Harvey Goldberg, who have written the three best accounts of the life of Jaurès, skillfully trace the lofty foreign policy concepts of the Great Tribune from his entry into the Chamber of Deputies in 1885 to his untimely assassination in 1914. They paint a warm and dramatic picture of a compassionate intellectual struggling against the primitive tribalism that finally plunged Europe into a bloody war. But their narratives are understandably one-sided, and they fail to provide a clear perspective of the overall foreign policy of the party, which by 1914 formed the second largest group in the Chamber of Deputies.

This study endeavors to narrow this gap by an examination of socialist foreign policy speeches and voting patterns in the Chamber of Deputies from the creation of the Anglo-French entente in 1904 to the outbreak of war in 1914. The year 1904 is a suitable starting point for two reasons. First, in that year negotiations were begun between the divided socialist parties that culminated in their unity in 1905. Second, the years 1904 to 1914 constitute a separate entity in European history. During those ten fateful years the forces of nationalism and imperialism brought to a head the tensions that had been building up since the end of the Franco-Prussian War of 1870-71, and in the end the Old World crumbled helplessly.

An examination of socialist foreign policy attitudes in the Chamber of Deputies requires more than an analysis of the parliamentary debates. Other sources, including the party congresses and the largest party newspaper, *Humanité*, have also

2

been utilized; for socialist foreign policy attitudes expressed in the Chamber often reflected ideas formulated outside the halls of parliament by personal conversations, newspaper editorials, caucuses of the socialist deputies, public demonstrations, and debates at party congresses. Nor can one divorce French socialist reaction to European events from developments within the Second International, whose views and actions often influenced the party's attitudes.

The road to the unity and parliamentary power traveled by the French socialists from 1870 to 1914 was long and tortuous. The brutal suppression of the Paris Commune in 1871 staggered the French labor movement, depriving it of such leaders as Jules Guesde, Jean Allemane, Paul Brousse, and Edouard Vaillant, who fled the country to escape execution or imprisonment. The successful repression of most socialist activity for the next five years seemed to indicate that socialism in France was dead.

In time, however, the passions engendered by the Commune faded. In 1876 the youthful Third Republic, confident in its ability to withstand political opposition, lifted the ban on socialist agitation. The tattered remnants of socialist leadership slowly wandered home. Jules Guesde returned from Switzerland and immediately attempted to reconstruct the debilitated movement. Within three years this ardent Marxist had consolidated a small number of collectivists into the French Workers' Party.

Small and isolated though it was, the socialist movement nevertheless suffered from doctrinal controversy and personality clashes. In October 1881 the pre-Commune followers of Auguste Blanqui, led by Communards like Edouard Vaillant and Emile Eudes, formed the Central Revolutionary Committee. The Blanquists accepted Marxian collectivism, but they differed from the Guesdists in their belief that the emancipation of the proletariat would be accomplished, not by a mass uprising of that class, but by the leadership of a small conspiratorial group. The next year

3

another Communard, Paul Brousse, leader of the reformist wing of Guesde's party, broke away and formed the Federation of Socialist Workers. These "Possibilists" emphasized parliamentary action, rather than revolution, to attain the socialist state. In 1890 the left wing of Brousse's party, led by another Communard, Jean Allemane, broke with the Possibilists to create the Revolutionary Socialist Workers' Party. Although the Allemanists accepted parliamentary methods, they also stressed revolution as a legitimate means to capture political power. By 1893 still another faction arose calling itself the Socialist Republican Federation of the Seine. This loose federation attracted hitherto uncommitted socialists, sometimes called "Independents." It was led primarily by men like René Viviani, Benoît Malon, Alexandre Millerand, Gustave Rouanet, and Jean Jaurès, who rejected the doctrinaire approach of the other four groups.[3]

Strangely enough, these divisions did not paralyze the socialist movement. Its doctrines appealed to a significant portion of a working class suffering from the economic depression of the 1880's. In the legislative elections of 1893 socialist candidates polled 598,000 of the 7,038,000 votes cast, and gained 37 of the 566 seats in the Chamber of Deputies. This impressive victory marked the birth of the socialist party as a major political force in the Third Republic.[4]

The newly elected socialist deputies made the first of many attempts to unify the dissenting factions. They formed the Socialist Union to coordinate their efforts in the struggle against capitalism; and they pledged support to Alexandre Millerand's Saint-Mandé Program of 1896, the classical statement of revisionist socialism emphasizing the principle of collectivization by gradual, electoral means.[5]

Two years later France was torn apart by the Dreyfus Affair. In the political and social turmoil of 1898 the socialists, believing that clerical and military forces threatened the Republic, created a Committee of Vigilance to present a united front to the forces of reaction. In the elections of that year additional parliamentary strength was added to this newfound unity. Socialist candidates received 880,000 of the 7,828,000 votes cast, raising their number of seats in the Chamber to forty-two.

But the unity created by the Dreyfus Affair was short-lived. In 1899 René Waldeck-Rousseau, Moderate senator for the Loire, created a broadly based Ministry of Republican Defense in an effort to restore order out of the chaos of the Affair. Seeking socialist support, he selected Millerand as minister of commerce. Millerand's collaboration with a bourgeois government incensed the Guesdists and Blanquists, especially when they learned that the new premier had chosen General Gaston Galliffet as minister of war. The socialists loathed Galliffet for his role in the suppression of the Commune. Although Jaurès and many Independents argued that the danger to the Republic justified Millerand's acceptance of a ministerial post, the presence of a socialist in the same ministry with the "butcher of the Communards" opened old wounds, and the Guesdists and Blanquists withdrew from the Socialist Union.

The debate over Millerand and ministerialism was carried to the First General Congress of French Socialist Organizations, held at Paris the following December. There the delegates passed a contradicatory resolution, condemning ministerialism yet declaring that under "exceptional circumstances" it might be permitted. This compromise might have patched up socialist differences, but six months later a strike at Chalon-sur-Saône, during which gendarmes killed several workers, revived the debate. The Guesdists and Blanquists demanded a parliamentary investigation; but the Possibilists, Allemanists, and Independents, unwilling to offend the ministry of which Millerand was a part, refused to support the Guesdist demand. The Guesdists considered this a betrayal of the workers; and at the second national congress of the federated groups (Paris, September 1900) the Guesdists, failing to obtain an unequivocal condemnation of ministerialism, walked out of the congress and formed the Socialist Party of France, which the Blanquists joined the next year. Meanwhile, Jaurès assumed leadership of the federated groups, which became the French Socialist Party.

Despite this bitter feud, socialist candidates continued to gain at the polls. In the elections of 1902 they polled over 900,000 of 8,412,000 votes cast, and won forty-eight seats in the Chamber. The following June, Waldeck-Rousseau, after an unprecedented two years as president of the Council, resigned for reasons of health. The Radical senator Emile Combes formed a new and more pronouncedly anticlerical government dedicated to educational reform, abolition of the religious orders, and separation of Church and State. The thirty-two deputies of Jaurès's party supported Combes's program, but the twelve members of the Socialist Party of France refused to collaborate with the bourgeois ministry and united in the Revolutionary Socialist Union.[6]

The impetus to unity between these two parties came from the Second International. In August 1904 the Sixth Congress of the Socialist and Labor International, meeting at Amsterdam, passed the Rheims-Dresden Resolution, which condemned socialist participation in bourgeois parliamentary blocks. This resolution urged the French socialists to create a united Marxist party in order to combat the reactionary policies of bourgeois governments in domestic and foreign affairs. After a hard fight Jaurès bowed to the decision of the Second International in the hope of achieving French socialist unity. Negotiations were begun between the two parties in September; and after twenty-eight years of division the French socialists united, in April of 1905, as the Socialist Party, French Section of the Workers' International (*Parti Socialiste, Section Française de l'Internationale Ouvrière*—SFIO).[7]

Before this epochal consolidation, foreign policy had remained secondary to the French parliamentary socialists. Internal division and preoccupation with domestic matters had diverted their attention from the international scene,[8] and the foreign policy ideas they occasionally had set forth lacked both clarity and sophistication. Each of the five factions had formulated certain basic attitudes toward patriotism, internationalism, and militarism, however; and an understanding of these is essential in order to understand the foreign policy that evolved in the united party.

Few pre-Commune French Marxists had fully accepted the concept of national defense. During the 1880's, however, many socialists began to view the Republic as a means to attain socialist ends. Socialist acceptance of the Third Republic was not the product of a hard-core pragmatism; it was essentially an acceptance of the French republican tradition based upon a double heritage of the French Revolution.

Two prevailing ideas had emerged from that nonsocialist revolution. The first was the principle of individual liberty, an important theme in the cosmopolitan literature and philosophy of the eighteenth century, especially in that of Rousseau and Montesquieu, and in the Declaration of the Rights of Man. The second was the notion of the nation as the collective embodiment and safeguard of that liberty. This concept, influencing socialist attitudes toward national defense and armament, emanated from the wars of the revolution that had produced Jacobin nationalism and the idea of the sanctity of the nation-state. To the socialists of the late nineteenth and early twentieth centuries the defense of France meant the defense of liberty and human progress. This patriotism, from Babeuf to Jaurès, was "defensive" and derived from Jacobin principles. Thus, the socialists, subscribing to the principles of the constitutions of 1791 and 1793, viewed a professional standing army as the last stronghold of despotism, the instrument with which to wage wars of aggression and colonial campaigns. In its stead they favored the general armament of all citizens, as in 1793, to protect France.[9]

The Guesdists supported these principles. In their party program of 1882 they advocated the abolition of professional standing armies and the creation of a national militia.[10] They argued that the professional army was ineffectual for national defense and that the reason for its existence was defense of the capitalist order. The Guesdist Paul Lafargue, son-in-law of Karl Marx, wrote that the French army did not "look toward the frontier, but toward the workshops. . . . Its only goal . . . is the defense of the capitalist bourgeoisie and its leaders."[11] During the parliament of 1889-93 the Guesdist deputies expressed this sentiment by proposing a motion to prohibit the intervention of troops in conflicts between capital and labor.[12]

On the other hand, the Guesdists accepted national patriotism. The National Council of the French Workers' Party expressed the patriotic attitudes of most Guesdists in a manifesto on "Patriotism and Socialism" published in January 1893. This manifesto advocated a kind of workers' international patriotism and declared *la patrie* "a necessary step toward human unity," adding that "because we are patriots we do not wish war."[13] Shortly before the elections of 1893 another manifesto affirmed that "the French Workers' Party is the only true patriotic party."[14] At their eleventh national congress (Paris, October 1893) the delegates agreed that the worker had the right and the duty to defend his country against any aggressor, and they expressed this view by stating that "if France were attacked it would have no more ardent defenders than the socialists of the Workers' Party."[15]

The Allemanists were the most vociferous internationalists and antimilitarists among the five factions. At their congress in 1891 (Paris) they adopted a motion attacking standing armies and urging opposition to war by abstention or revolt. Their propaganda became one of the chief inspirations of the idea of a general strike to prevent war.[16] As opposed to the Allemanists, the Possibilists rejected antipatriotism, even though they, too, called for the abolition of permanent armies and urged the collaboration of the workers of Europe.[17]

The Blanquists, who worked closely with the Guesdists, evade accurate description. Their concept of a revolutionary, conspiratorial elite resembled that of the Leninists of the Russian Revolution.[18] With its tradition of insurrection, Blanquism was more a state of mind than a political doctrine. After the death of Blanqui in 1881, however, Edouard Vaillant assumed leadership of the Central Revolutionary Committee, and the Blanquists became more and more characterized by a strong pacifism and internationalism. In 1881 they instituted a league "for the suppression of permanent armies and their replacement by a national militia."[19] The next year the Blanquist deputy Jules Gambon proposed to the Chamber of Deputies a law for the suppression of standing armies, and Vaillant presented a similar motion in 1894.[20]

The Independent socialists likewise denounced standing armies, although they were energetic supporters of the Republic. In the Saint-Mandé Program, Millerand insisted that "while we are internationalists we are also Frenchmen and patriots."[21] Another leading Independent, Benoît Malon, often criticized the professional standing army as the chief cause of war and advocated that a federation of all the European nations could achieve a lasting peace.[22]

Among all the socialists before 1905, the Independent Jaurès was the most persistent and experienced foreign policy observer. He kept a watchful eye on international developments and consistently expressed his foreign policy views in the socialist newspapers *Petite République*, *Dépêche de Toulouse*, and *Humanité*. These articles, published by Max Bonnafous in 1931 under the title *Pour la paix*, revealed a strong opposition to armaments, colonialism, and the Franco-Russian Alliance in favor of a mixture of pacifism and patriotism imbued with the memories of 1789 and conditioned by the goal of a social republic.[23] These ideas reflected in substance the ideas of the majority of French socialists.[24]

Jaurès's early foreign policy views concerned the Franco-Russian Alliance and the condition of suppressed peoples in the colonial areas. Before 1890 he had been hostile to Czarist Russia; but in the *Dépêche de Toulouse* of August 6, 1891, he praised the recent rapprochement between France and Russia and even defended the Russian monarchy as "the soul of the Russian people," as opposed to the "unpopular" monarchies of Germany, Austria-Hungary, and Italy.[25] During the ministry of Jules Méline (1896-98) Jaurès reverted to his earlier hostility toward Czarism when, in the *Petite République* of July 27, 1897, he accused Méline of selling France to the Russian Empire.[26] This became Jaurès's lifelong attitude, and it placed him in consistent opposition to one of the guiding principles of French foreign policy.

Jaurès considered colonial expansion to be a "natural law," but he believed that socialists should strive to ensure that colonial competition never resulted in war and that the natives of the colonizing areas were protected from abuse.[27] In 1896 Jaurès expressed horror, in both the Chamber and the press, at the massacres in Armenia; and during the revolt of Crete the next year, he continued his defense of oppressed peoples with an impassioned plea for Cretan self-determination.[28] During the Fashoda crisis of 1898 he demanded that France abandon Fashoda; and in a series of articles on Anglo-French relations in the *Petite République*, he attacked both English and French chauvinism and imperialism, which he pictured as the inevitable results of capitalism.[29] During the Boer War of 1899 he praised the resistance of the Boers, but he denounced the nationalists who advocated an anti-English alliance of France, Russia, and Germany.[30] Between 1893 and 1905 Jaurès's foreign policy attitudes were based essentially upon a vision of a humane and just society inaugurated by the international proletariat. These

10

attitudes, based as they were upon Jacobin principles and liberal humanitarianism, had departed a long way from the rigid doctrines of Marxism.

Thus, up to this point the French socialists had formulated a variety of recurrent opinions on foreign policy matters, but no systematic approach. They detested the Franco-Russian Alliance, armaments, colonial excesses, and professional standing armies. Between 1904 and 1914, however, foreign policy matters became their foremost concern. In the Chamber of Deputies from October 1904 to December 1906, almost half of the speeches by socialist deputies were devoted to militarism, internationalism, national defense, and more specific problems of foreign policy. From January 1907 to May 1911 the socialists divided their attention about equally between foreign policy matters and the numerous strikes that plagued France during the ministries of Georges Clemenceau (1906-9) and Aristide Briand (1909-11). From July 1911 to the outbreak of war in August 1914, nearly two thirds of the speeches by socialist deputies were concerned with foreign and military affairs.

This abrupt change in emphasis was prompted by two factors. The resolution of their internal division allowed the socialists to give more attention to foreign policy issues, and the threatening nature of the international situation itself compelled them to define their attitudes clearly. In 1904, after a five-year period of relative quiet, European tensions were increasing. The next two years were a sort of dress rehearsal for 1914. They contained all the major elements, with the exception of the Balkan problem, that were present in the crisis that finally destroyed Old Europe—including the armaments race, Far Eastern rivalries, the play of alliances, trade and investment competition, and the desire for colonial acquisition.[31] With the Austrian annexation of Bosnia and Herzegovina in the fall of 1908, Austro-Russian rivalry in the Balkans got under way, while the continued Franco-German rivalry in Morocco also threatened the delicate peace. Between 1911 and 1914 Europe suffered through still another Moroccan crisis, the Italian war against Turkey, and the two Balkan Wars. Anglo-German naval competition continued to increase, and both Germany and France enlarged their armies to prepare for the moment of truth.

An analysis of the French socialist reaction to the critical events of this period must seek to answer several questions. What were the principles upon which the parliamentary socialists based their approach to foreign policy issues? In facing the international problems of the time, did the socialists always abide by these principles; and if not, what were the forces that led them to change their attitudes? The fact that the socialists were unified upon the Marxian principles of the Rheims-Dresden Resolution raises further questions. Did the socialists approach foreign affairs in a unified spirit of Marxian internationalism? What was the role of the revisionist Jaurès in a party supposedly organized along Marxist lines, and what part did patriotism and pacifism play in the united party? Were there any reflections in socialist comments on foreign policy of the separate groupings that existed before 1905? What was the nature of the relations of the united party with the Second International, especially with the German socialists? Finally, and more important, did the foreign policy of the French parliamentary socialists exert any effective influence upon the course of French foreign policy before World War I?

NATIONAL DEFENSE,

FRANCO-GERMAN RAPPROCHEMENT,

AND THE NEW ARMY

During the years from 1904 to 1914, French socialist attitudes toward national defense formed the basis of French socialist foreign policy. These attitudes are characterized by certain major principles that manifested themselves in almost every socialist foreign policy speech. Jaurès defined these in the Chamber of Deputies on December 8, 1905, when he explained that the foreign policy of his party was based upon four major aims: (1) to uphold the defensive power of the nation; (2) to adjust military policy to the conditions of life in a democracy; (3) to unify all countries by the collective action of the proletariat; and (4) to support all efforts of the government of

France to resolve international problems by arbitration.[1] The socialist leader reviewed these principles on January 13, 1911, when he told the Chamber that socialist foreign policy was determined by three important objectives: (1) to maintain freedom of French international action to serve the cause of peace, despite the binding clauses of secret agreements; (2) to transform the forces of finance and credit into servants and not masters of French foreign policy; and (3) to lift France to a position of moral leadership in the world in order to bring peace and justice to oppressed peoples.[2]

A study of socialist action in the Chamber of Deputies on national defense reveals the extent of socialist agreement with these principles. The majority of the socialists rejected extreme antimilitarism and maintained a willingness to defend France against aggressors. A concept of "defensive patriotism" provided the basis for their foreign policy views. The Third Republic was the logical development of the ideals of the French Revolution; and while the socialists might advocate the disarmament of all nations, they insisted that France, the nation they believed to be the birthplace of human freedom and justice, be kept strong.

French socialist patriotism represented essentially the typical middle-class attitude toward *la patrie*. The great majority of the socialist deputies, many of whom had joined the party on intellectual and humanitarian grounds, were doctors, lawyers, and professors. Among the 54 socialists elected to the Chamber of Deputies in 1906, for example, there were 38 professional men and 7 journalists, while only 9 of the deputies could claim to belong to the laboring class. Edouard Vaillant and Paul Brousse were doctors of medicine. Francis de Pressensé and Jaurès were professors, although they, like Jules Guesde, Gustave Rouanet, Marcel Sembat, and a large number of the lawyers, engaged in part- or full-time journalism after having entered politics. Among those socialist deputies with working-class backgrounds, Jean Allemane had been a printer before his participation in the Commune.[3]

Despite this impressive membership of men who had affirmed their loyalty to the Republic during the critical months of the Dreyfus Affair and during the Combes era, many members of the Right feared this new and supposedly Marxist party as a grave threat to national security. On December 1, 1905, the SFIO was charged with promoting antimilitarism among the Bourses du Travail and encouraging treason and anarchy in the army. After the socialist deputies Maurice Allard (Var), Albert Carnaud (Bouches-du-Rhône), Adrien Meslier (Seine), and Arthur Lamendin (Pas-de-Calais) had brandished their patriotism in replying to these charges, Jules Coutant, a former Blanquist and deputy for the Seine, insisted that the parliamentary socialists considered patriotism and internationalism to be complementary. Marcel Sembat, another former Blanquist, a writer for *Humanité*, and deputy for the Seine, explained that the small minority of socialists who advocated insurrection in case of war were not representative of the parliamentary group.[4] When the debate was resumed one week later, Alexandre Zévaès, Independent socialist deputy for Isère and an important historian of the French socialist movement, fervently and vehemently defended French socialist patriotism and drew lively applause as he declared: "If France were threatened by an invader . . . the French socialists would, to their last breath, defend the last inch of soil where liberty was born and social justice nurtured."[5]

Such profuse affirmations of loyalty to France failed to banish the fears of the Right. On March 6, 1906, the Radical deputy Lucien Klotz, long known for his vociferous expressions of anti-German sentiment, joined the Right in a vicious attack on socialist patriotism. Labeling the socialists as "demagogues of peace," he charged that their pacifist theories were undermining the military forces that conserved peace. When he reminded the Extreme Left that it had not voted for the war budget of 1906, Paul Constans, socialist deputy for Allier, and Victor Dejeante, secretary of the SFIO and deputy for the Seine, retorted that their party would never vote for a bourgeois budget that was leading France to an inevitable war.[6] In June 1908 the socialists again came under heavy fire from the Right when they criticized the government for dismissing a public school teacher, Roux Castadau, for teaching antimilitarist ideas.[7] After another such attack the following November, Francis de Pressensé, socialist deputy for the Rhône, son of a Protestant clergyman, and one of the numerous intellectuals attracted to socialism during the Dreyfus Affair, spoke for his party when he affirmed that the SFIO would do all within its power to prevent war, but that "if the day comes when there is a necessary, legitimate war, provoked unjustly, the proletariat and its leaders will be the first to support France."[8] Nevertheless, the Marquis de Dion, nationalist deputy for Loire-Inférieure, grew so fearful of socialist internationalism that in May 1909 he proposed—unsuccessfully, amid laughs and taunts from socialist benches—that the singing of the socialist anthem, "The Internationale," be outlawed.[9]

The socialists invariably reacted to these attacks by proclaiming the SFIO to be the only true patriotic party in France. Jean Bouveri, socialist deputy for Saône-et-Loire and former secretary of the Miners Union at Montceau, assured the Chamber on October 27, 1910, that the socialists were devoted to the Republic. He brushed aside as foolishness the accusations of the Marquis de Dion and of Baudry d'Asson, royalist deputy for Vendée, that his party was attempting to convert the strikes of 1910 into full-scale insurrection.[10] Maurice Allard argued in *Humanité* that the socialists, who opposed war and conquest, were the only true patriots; the real antipatriots were the chauvinists or "professional patriots," bent upon a destructive war, and the capitalists and financiers, who placed their own interests above those of the nation.[11] Gustave Rouanet, deputy for the

16

Seine, likewise pictured the SFIO as the only real patriotic party because it represented the interests of the proletariat, and Paul Lafargue, who was a member of the Permanent Administrative Commission of the party, ridiculed the *sans-patrie* bourgeoisie that never had the interests of France at heart.[12]

Thus, the socialists' insistence upon their patriotism was often a defensive reaction to charges that the SFIO was inciting the workers to revolution and the soldiers to desertion. Socialist devotion to the Republic, as pointed out earlier, was genuine. But many historians, in an eagerness to emphasize this patriotism, have distorted the picture by overlooking the context in which these patriotic utterances were made. The French socialists may have protested excessively in order to justify a pacifism that did in fact exist. They were committed to a program of effective national defense, but it was a program based upon "an exclusively defensive foreign policy."[13] Faithful to their pre-1905 hostility to professional standing armies, they believed that such a pacifist foreign policy should center around a citizen army. They argued that a small professional army had been used in the past as an instrument to maintain the bourgeoisie in power and to wage wars of colonial aggression. In addition, they doubted its ability to stave off a German onslaught.

On March 1, 1906, Jean Bouhey-Allex, socialist deputy for Côte-d'Or and a former army officer cashiered in 1894 because of his socialist opinions, pleaded for the creation of a true national army by means of an expanded reserve system composed of all citizens. He pointed to the waste and inadequacy of French defenses and accused military leaders of clinging to moribund military tactics. The system of fortifications, he claimed, had not kept pace with the progress of artillery. He predicted that if war should come, Germany would simply ignore these inadequate fortifications and invade France through neutral Belgium. To cope with such an eventuality, the nation should create a system of rapid mobilization whereby it could pass to a war-footing in twenty-four hours. This was possible only by the creation of a force of armed citizens on instant call in a strengthened reserve.[14]

In November of the next year Alexandre Varenne, socialist deputy for Puy-de-Dôme, a lawyer, and a part-time journalist for the socialist newspaper *Lanterne*, called for further military reforms. Supported by Jean Allemane (Seine), Félix Aldy (Aude), Pierre Colliard (Rhône), and Albert Willm (Seine), he stressed that effective national defense demanded that France have a more rapid mobilization and troop transportation scheme. He also suggested that young soldiers serve their time at the military post nearest their homes so that "on the day of mobilization" France would be defended by "resolute young men, conscious of their duty and ready to carry it out."[15] On December 21, 1908, Jaurès criticized the overall condition of the nation's defenses, especially in the disorganization of the French artillery system; and he, too, called for the creation of a citizen army by means of a strengthened reserve.[16] The next day Allemane and Gäetan Albert-Poulain (Ardennes) stressed that France could defend itself against Germany only if it reorganized the entire army into a national militia.[17]

The nationalists who questioned socialist support of national defense wrongly identified the extreme antimilitarist activities of a minority outside the parliament with the patriotic ideas of the parliamentary group. The inspiration of this minority in the SFIO was Gustave Hervé, a former instructor of history at the lycées of Rodez, Alençon, and Sens, prominent among the Independents after 1902. In 1904 he fell under the influence of revolutionary syndicalism. He joined the SFIO in 1905, but he continued to expound his intense antipatriotic views in his weekly newspaper, *La Guerre sociale*, founded the next year. In his principal work, *Leur patrie*, published in 1904, Hervé accused the parliamentary socialists of failing to preserve the revolutionary purity of socialist doctrines of international-

18

ism.[18] In September 1907 Hervé was sentenced to eleven years in prison for his antipatriotic propaganda.[19]

Many socialist leaders, while disagreeing with Hervé's ideas, defended his right to proclaim them and protested his imprisonment. Edouard Vaillant, deputy for the Seine, and Marcel Sembat defended him at his trial.[20] Jaurès termed his sentence "brutal,"[21] and Jules Uhry, a member of the National Council of the party and a reporter for *Humanité*, labeled the court an "inquisition."[22] In the Chamber of Deputies on March 30, 1908, Sembat, Constans, and Willm requested that Hervé be included in an amnesty for those arrested during the Midi strikes of 1908. Although their request was rejected by a vote of 439 to 70,[23] Hervé was released a few months later.

Hervé, as champion of the general strike and insurrection in case of war, confronted the united party with the challenge of revolutionary syndicalism, which he believed best combined the traditions of Marx and the anarchist Bakunin.[24] But the party rejected the intense antipatriotism and antimilitarism of Hervé, while the syndicalist General Confederation of Labor in turn castigated the socialists as "counterfeiters of the great socialist idea."[25] The leaders of the SFIO and the General Confederation of Labor seldom collaborated on foreign policy matters during this period, with the exception of occasional joint efforts in the organization of peace rallies or the issuing of peace manifestos. The two groups, for example, joined in organizing a peace demonstration at Paris on September 14, 1911, during the Agadir crisis; and during the socialist campaign against the three-year law they sponsored an antiwar rally of 150,000 at Pré-Saint-Gervais on May 25, 1913.[26]

Many French socialists, fearing that Hervé's propaganda would hurt the party, openly condemned his heresy. In 1906 a group of former Possibilists, led by Paul Brousse, protested to the National Council that Hervé's extremism was discrediting socialism.[27] The next year the National Council censured Hervé for his frequent and vitriolic attacks in *La Guerre sociale* on the patriotic ideas of the parliamentary socialists, who, according to Hervé, had betrayed the socialist ideal by attempting "to join internationalism and patriotism, class struggle and class communion in love of a common fatherland."[28] Gustave Rouanet exhorted the party to disavow any relationship with the antimilitarists;[29] and at the national party congresses at Limoges (1906) and Nancy (1907) Jaurès, Vaillant, and Guesde led the majority in condemning the partisans of insurrection.[30]

Jaurès opposed Hervé's motions on insurrection at the party congresses, for he knew that an endorsement of extreme antimilitarism would discredit the SFIO in the eyes of the workers. Yet his attitude toward Hervé remained ambivalent. While he lamented that Hervé's extremist propaganda had provoked the charge of *sans-patrie* against the socialists and feared that Hervé's sentence in 1907 lent "moral authority to his ideas, many of which are disreputable,"[31] Jaurès was tolerant of dissenting viewpoints. Aside from the debates over insurrection at the party congresses, where he knew that the future electoral success of the party was at stake, he refused to condemn Hervé outright. He also recognized the growing strain of pacifism in the party and feared that an unequivocal condemnation of Hervéism might cause a party rift.

By his refusal to condemn Hervéism forthrightly, Jaurès, as leader of the patriotic majority, strengthened the impression among outsiders that Hervé's ideas, which attracted attention both in France and abroad, represented those of the party. Thus, the respected conservative *Journal des débats* could speak of "the conversion of Jaurès to Hervéism,"[32] and Philip Lavino, Paris correspondent of the London *Times*, made no distinction between Hervé's and Jaurès's ideas in his daily reports to English readers on political activities in France.[33] The poet Charles Péguy, in 1909, attacked "demagogic Hervéism" and mourned "this unbelievable, perpetual capitulation of Jaurès to Hervé," contending that "without Jaurès, Hervé is nothing. By Jaurès he becomes authorized, he becomes authentic."[34]

Hervé's agitation, extreme and unreasonable though it was, at least drew public attention to the question of socialist conduct in case of war and thus compelled the SFIO to deal with the problem more thoroughly. This it did at party congresses and at the congresses of the Second International. At the third national congress of the SFIO (Limoges, November 1-4, 1906), when Hervé called for insurrection in case of war, Guesde opposed the motion, arguing that if the socialists undermined national defense by calling a strike in the event of war, they would be delivering "the most socialist nation on earth" to a nonsocialist enemy. He contended that the proletariat should not waste time on insurrection; it should rather capture political power in order to combat the chief cause of war—capitalism.[35]

Guesde's ideas represented a trend of thought in the SFIO distinct from either the minority of Hervé or the majority of Vaillant and Jaurès. Faithful to Marxian logic, Guesde believed war to be the inevitable consequence of the capitalist order. He urged the socialists to remember that their chief struggle was against capitalism rather than against war. His ideas in this respect, however, were inconsistent. On the one hand, he had often preached, as during the Anglo-Russian crisis of 1885, that war was not only inevitable in the capitalist order but also desirable as a means of hastening social revolution.[36] On the other hand, he maintained, as at Limoges, that socialists should not undermine national defense by insurrection. His professed Marxian internationalism could not overcome his belief in the duty of the citizen to defend France, a duty he had emphasized when the Republic seemed threatened during the Dreyfus Affair of 1898. Guesde's ideas, though eloquently expressed at the party congresses, attracted even fewer followers than Hervé's.

Jaurès and Vaillant carried the majority at Limoges. Their motion was composed of two contradictory parts, illustrating the socialist dilemma. The first part condemned militarism and imperialism, but emphasized the right and duty of the citizen to defend France against an unprovoked attack. The second part expressed solidarity with the workers of all nations and resolved to use all possible means to prevent war, from "parliamentary intervention, public agitation, and popular manifestations, to the general strike and insurrection."[37]

The next party congress at Nancy (August 11-14, 1907) was almost a repetition of the congress at Limoges. Hervé demanded that the previous year's motion be amended to include a definite commitment to the general strike in the event of war. Guesde again rejected Hervé's arguments, but he also ridiculed the revisionist motion. The second clause declaring that socialists would use all possible means to prevent war was pacifist, he argued, while the first clause stating that the proletariat should defend France against an aggressor was "superpatriotic."[38]

Guesde's well-reasoned argument had little effect on the majority of the delegates. Vaillant stressed the possibility of bilateral French and German socialist action in case of war; and Jaurès, affirming his adherence to the Limoges resolution, found himself in the ironic position of being to the left of the Marxist Guesde in international affairs. The majority then followed the deputy for the Tarn, who termed Hervé's motion "confusing and dangerous." The congress reaffirmed its stand of the previous year after rejecting Hervé's amendment by a vote of 251 to 41.[39]

Hervé did not give up. A few days later he carried his arguments to the seventh congress of the Second International (Stuttgart), again calling for insurrection and the general strike in case of war. The leader of the German delegation, August Bebel, unwilling to jeopardize the position of his party at home by adopting a controversial motion which he considered unrealistic anyway, rejected Hervé's arguments. He argued that the Second International need only reaffirm the resolutions on war it had passed at Zurich (1893) and Paris (1900). Both of these

22

motions instructed socialists to use all possible means to prevent war, while conceding that the proletariat should defend its homeland in case of attack. Guesde intervened with his traditional arguments, but Jaurès and Vaillant presented a motion that pleased everyone. Their motion failed to mention the general strike; but it declared that if war broke out, socialists should strive to bring it to an end and use the resulting political and economic chaos to overthrow capitalist class rule.[40]

The motions of the party after Stuttgart assumed a more pacifist tone each year, not pacifist in the sense of outright refusal to bear arms, even in defense of the country, but in the sense that the socialists turned their attention more and more to the problems of militarism and war and accelerated their efforts to achieve an unarmed world through international arbitration. The delegates to the fifth national congress of the SFIO (Toulouse, October 15-18, 1908) warned that the proletariat would not tolerate continuing increases in armaments.[41] Two years later, at their national congress at Paris, the socialists condemned chauvinism and urged French and German disarmament.[42] The next month, at the eighth congress of the Second International (Copenhagen), Vaillant, with the approval of the French delegation, and James Keir Hardie, the veteran of the British labor movement, submitted an amendment to the Stuttgart resolution calling for a strike of transports, mines, and arsenals to paralyze mobilization in case of war. But the International congress, led again by the German socialists, merely reaffirmed the Stuttgart resolution.[43]

The growing strength of pacifism in the SFIO in the years immediately preceding the war was closely related to the increasing acceptance by the French socialists of the general strike as a means to prevent war, as at the Copenhagen congress in 1910. One is tempted to attribute this new pacifist tone to the influence of Hervé. Indeed, the agitation of his followers in the Yonne, where the extreme antimilitarist propaganda of the pre-1905 Allemanists had prepared the ground for Hervéism, did plant within the SFIO the idea of the general strike as a means to prevent war. Though a minority, the former Allemanists within the united party were a vociferous group; and support for Hervé's motions on insurrection came mostly from those federations where the Allemanists had been strongest,[44] thus revealing a reflection of the pre-1905 disunity. But the exact degree of Hervé's influence on the peace motions of the party is difficult to determine. At the 1910 party congress at Paris, just a few days before Vaillant proposed his amendment to the Stuttgart resolution at Copenhagen, Hervé had again proposed a motion calling for insurrection in case of war, and this motion had received only 34 out of a total of 244 votes.[45]

Hervé's continued defeats are easily explained. Many French socialists disliked Hervé because of his incessant attacks upon the revolutionary purity of the party; many disliked him because of his radical brand of antimilitarism, which they realized was an affront to the deep patriotism of the average worker. Hervé was generally unpopular among all classes of the French population. The socialist attitude was therefore an exercise in political realism. In any case, Hervé experienced a private change of heart in 1912, becoming a supporter of Republican defense and a correspondingly more tractable member of the SFIO. In 1914 he volunteered for frontline duty. His effect on the discussions at the party congresses found no parallels in parliament or at the polls, where socialist disregard of his proposals may have contributed to the continuing growth of the movement's strength.

The French socialists' acceptance of the general strike, on the other hand, resulted from the threatening international situation. The socialists recognized the threat of war in Morocco and in the Balkans; but their proposals to safeguard the peace, such as their persistent pleas that French troops be withdrawn from Morocco in order to avoid conflict with Germany and their

24

constructive suggestion that the Powers create a Balkan federation in order to resolve Austro-Russian rivalry, were consistently defeated. Their only weapon appeared to be the threat of a paralyzing counterstroke that would prevent the capitalists from sending the sons of the workers to their death.

There was still another factor that contributed to French socialist approval of the general strike. The delegates to the eleventh national party congress (Amiens, January 25-28, 1914) agreed that in the coming legislative elections of April and May the party would support on the second ballot any Radical or Radical-Socialist who favored repeal of a law passed in 1913 which had raised military service from two to three years.[46] Such collaboration with bourgeois parties violated the pact of unity and the party's revolutionary tradition. Approval of the general strike to prevent war was thus one way to redress the balance and to pacify the socialist conscience.

In the Chamber of Deputies the pacifism of the party found its greatest expression in the struggle against armaments and militarism and in the campaign for international arbitration and a Franco-German rapprochement. Between 1905 and 1914 the socialists voted unanimously against the annual budgets, arguing that they contained excessive military expenditures and ignored social legislation. Only once, in 1907, did a party member, Jules-Louis Breton, deputy for the Cher (who left the party in 1912), vote for the budget; and at the next party congress at Toulouse he was threatened with expulsion.[47]

The parliamentary socialists, as pointed out earlier, supported effective land defense by means of a national militia to be used only in case of invasion. But they opposed buildups in naval armaments, arguing that they served an aggressive purpose and intensified international rivalry. On February 22, 1906, when Gaston Thomson, navy minister in Ferdinand Sarrien's government, proposed the construction of four additional battleships, Jaurès objected that the projected addition might encourage England, Germany, and Italy to accelerate their naval programs. The Chamber ignored Jaurès's arguments and approved the new constructions by a vote of 428 to 111.[48]

The following month Thomson proposed the additional construction of a new battleship comparable to the English *Dreadnought*.[49] A few days later he asked for additions to the French submarine fleet.[50] Debate on these proposals was begun on November 22, 1906, when Jaurès termed the naval program "a program of folly" and other socialists declared Thomson's plans to be "the road to destruction."[51] The next day Alexandre Varenne delivered a lengthy attack against naval armaments. He contended that further construction would be ruinous to French finances because the government had already spent over a billion francs for new construction and would undoubtedly request more; and as a result of these financial commitments, social legislation lagged. Varenne concluded by warning that the working class was becoming more and more unwilling to bear the burden of armed peace.[52] Again the Chamber rejected the arguments of the socialists by a vote of 379 to 112.[53]

The failure of the socialists' attack against armament increases did not undermine their belief in the possibility of eventual agreement among the Powers to end the alarming armaments race. They viewed the Hague Peace Conference of 1907 as a partial fulfillment of their hopes for an international force that could resolve disputes through arbitration. On June 7, 1907, Francis de Pressensé, while admitting that the Hague Conference would not produce a cure, praised it as a noble effort for peace. He warned that French indifference would be a crime against humanity and suggested that the French representatives to the Hague support England's proposal for a limitation of armaments.[54] François Fournier, Independent socialist for the Gard, recommended that France propose a constitution for an international parliament with a court of arbitration and a special code to regulate treaties of commerce.[55] The socialist deputies, especially Maurice Allard, deputy for the Var and founder of the newspaper *Petit Var*, voiced strong approval of Fournier's proposal, but the majority in the Chamber voted against it.[56]

The Hague Conference achieved few tangible and lasting results; and its failure may have contributed to the growing strength of pacifism in the party, as evidenced by the renewed vigor with which the socialists attacked armaments after 1907. The armed peace troubled the French socialists, and they blamed European tensions on profit-seeking industrialists and financiers. At their party congress at Nancy in 1907, the delegates commended the socialist deputies for their incessant struggle against the "international financiers who toy with the peace of the world and endlessly compromise it by their ruthless brigandage."[57] On the rostrum Jaurès often expressed fear that Europe had reached an impasse. Noting the enormous military budgets of the various Powers, he urged that France take the first step toward European disarmament by gradually cutting down its own military expenditures.[58] In January 1911 he lamented Europe's lack of faith in arbitration and ridiculed the idea of "vital interests and honor" to justify belligerent behavior. Arbitration had proved its worth during the Fashoda crisis of 1898, he reasoned, and it had worked when the United States intervened to help end the Russo-Japanese War. Jaurès then proposed a resolution exhorting the government to follow the lead of the United States in resolving all conflicts in this manner.[59] The next month Albert Emile Goude, the youthful socialist deputy for Finistère and former deputy-mayor of Brest, rose to make a similar case.[60] A few days later Sembat challenged the government's professed desire for peace by demanding that it proclaim formally its desire for an international concert of Powers to limit armaments; if France took the lead, he asserted, the other countries would follow. Foreign Minister Stéphen Pichon rejected Sembat's proposition, arguing that the best guarantee of peace was a strong army and navy.[61] The following month the socialist deputies Sixte Quenin (Bouches-du-Rhône), Raffin Dugens (Isère), and Jean Colly (Seine) bitterly criticized Pichon's reasoning, contending that it was foolish to assume that the best way to avoid war was to prepare for it.[62]

The socialist campaign against armaments and for international arbitration continued throughout the years just preceding the war. The French socialists fervently pleaded the cause of peace during the second Moroccan crisis and the Balkan Wars, and at their tenth national congress (Brest, March 23-25, 1913) they again condemned the armed peace as a detriment to European social and economic life.[63] Early in 1914 the parliamentary socialists pressed their antimilitarist campaign, applauding Albert Thomas, deputy for the Seine, for his virulent attack against increased armaments during a debate over additional naval funds.[64]

The pacifism of the French socialists also manifested itself in their pleas for reconciliation between France and Germany. They believed that a Franco-German rapprochement would inaugurate a new era of European peace. Pressensé made a good historical case for such a rapprochement when he told the Chamber on November 26, 1908, that "the permanent setback to our foreign policy for the last half century has been tension between France and Germany." The future of Europe, he said, depended upon the resolution of this needless enmity, which only a rational foreign policy could erase. He traced the origin of this tension, from the Thirty Years' War through the Napoleonic Wars to the battle of Sedan in 1870. The French socialists, he said, would never accept this perpetual hostility toward the fatherland of Bach, Goethe, Kant, Beethoven, Wagner, and Karl Marx.[65] In December 1909 Pressensé again stressed the need for Franco-German reconciliation, arguing that the balance of power was a guarantee of peace rather than a reason for perpetual animosity among nations.[66]

28

Jaurès refuted the idea that Franco-German rivalry was the product of a natural and inevitable hatred between Germans and Frenchmen. It was rather a by-product of Anglo-German rivalry that often caught France in the middle. In the Chamber of Deputies in January 1909, he asserted that this rivalry posed the greatest threat to peace, and he urged that France and Germany forget the past and assume leadership of the forces of peace in Europe.[67] The following November he again argued that Franco-German difficulties were "just a superficial manifestation of Anglo-German conflict," and he pointed to Anglo-German rivalry in the Far East to prove his point. Jaurès believed that this rivalry could be resolved by the creation of a three-power entente composed of Britain, France, and Germany.[68] These arguments, however, ignored many other sources of European tension of which Jaurès himself had often spoken, including Austro-Russian rivalry in the Balkans and Franco-German rivalry in Morocco.

The second Moroccan crisis convinced the socialists even more of the need for a Franco-German rapprochement. During the debates over ratification of the Franco-German treaty of 1911, Sembat, Vaillant, and Jaurès strongly emphasized this theme.[69] At the party congress at Brest in March of 1913, Vaillant and Adéodat Compère-Morel, deputy for the Gard, argued that human progress was impossible as long as France and Germany quarreled.[70] Shortly before the campaign against the three-year law in 1913, Sembat published a pamphlet entitled *Faites un roi, sinon faites la paix*, arguing that the Republic was incapable of fighting a war; for the sake of its own existence, therefore, it should pursue a policy of peace, the first condition of which was a Franco-German reconciliation.[71] During the crusade against the three-year law *Humanité* printed daily on its front page the major aims of French socialist foreign policy: international arbitration, a citizen army, and reconciliation between France and Germany.[72]

The socialist yearning for closer ties with Germany resulted not only from Franco-German tensions but also from the French socialist respect for the growing power of the German socialists. Jaurès detested Hohenzollern absolutism, accusing it of "entering into a struggle with all the liberal movements of modern Germany";[73] and he viewed the German government as "aristocratic, feudal, and militaristic" and the Pan-Germanists as a constant menace to world peace.[74] But Jaurès believed that the German Social Democratic Party (*Sozialdemokratische Partei Deutschlands*—SPD) was one of the most effective guarantees of peace in Europe and that Germany's future was in its hands; for "in the vast plan of European evolution" the democratization of Germany was an essential part.[75] When the German socialists polled 4,250,300 votes and gained 110 seats in the Reichstag elections of 1912, the French socialists received the news joyfully, demonstrating 10,000 strong at the Salle Wagram in Paris on March 30. Jaurès, Guesde, and Vaillant shared the platform with the Reichstag deputies Philipp Scheidemann and Georg Weill, who called for a Franco-German rapprochement.[76]

Jaurès demonstrated his confidence in the pacifist sentiment of the German socialists during a dispute with Charles Andler in early 1913. Andler, a member of the SFIO and a professor of German history at the Sorbonne, was the author of the five-hundred-page work *Les Origines du socialisme d'état en Allemagne*, published in 1897. In November and December of 1912 he published two articles in the magazine *L'Action nationale* on "Imperialistic Socialism in Modern Germany." Andler contended that the German socialists had gradually succumbed to militarist and imperialist influences, and he pointed to their halfhearted opposition to Kaiser Wilhelm's action at Agadir in 1911 and to their solidarity with the colonial and military policies of the German government. He charged that the writings of such party theoreticians as Gerhard Hildebrand,

Max Schippel, Ludwig Quessel, and Karl Leuthner had strengthened the spirit of nationalism within the SPD. Even Bebel, he
said, had declared at the SPD congress at Jena in 1911 that
"the watchword of the hour is not to disarm, but to increase
armaments."[77]

Although Andler was a close friend of Lucien Herr, the
socialist librarian of the Ecole Normale Supérieure who is said
to have converted Jaurès to socialism, Jaurès was driven to a
bitter rebuttal. Andler's well-documented arguments had been
reprinted by *Le Temps* and *L'Eclair*, furnishing ammunition to
the critics of socialism. In an article entitled *Citation fausse*,
which appeared in *Humanité* on March 4, 1913, Jaurès termed
Andler a "provider of all the poisonous invective against us."
He correctly pointed out that Andler had misquoted Bebel and
that the SPD leader had actually said that "the watchword of
the hour for the bourgeoisie is not to disarm, but to increase
armaments," and this in reference to the failure of the English
proposals at the Hague Conference to limit armaments. Jaurès
emphasized that the German socialists had attacked their government for rejecting these proposals.[78] In the Chamber on June
17, 1913, Jaurès again defended the German socialists, praising
them for their courageous opposition to militarism and imperialism.[79] Although Jaurès had exposed Andler's careless mis-
quoting of Bebel, his overall rebuttal was unconvincing. He
ignored Andler's charges against the SPD theoreticians; and his
optimistic praise of German socialist pacifism was a weak reply
to Andler's central argument, backed by specific examples, that
nationalism had captured the German socialist movement.

The majority of the French socialists shared Jaurès's confidence in the SPD. They knew that the solidarity of the Second
International depended upon agreement and understanding between the two largest socialist parties in Europe. Their hopes
seemed near fulfillment when the congress of the International
met at Basel, Switzerland, in November 1912. Both French and

German socialists pleaded for a new covenant of peace that would end the conflict in the Balkans.[80] At the Inter-parliamentary Conference of Berne in May 1913, they joined with liberal parliamentarians to approve a resolution condemning armaments and chauvinism and appealing for a world of peace through international arbitration and a Franco-German rapprochement. Jaurès and Sembat, backed by the French and German socialist delegates, added to this resolution the Bryan Resolution of the American secretary of state, William Jennings Bryan, which stated that nations on the verge of war should wait at least six months for a cooling-off period.[81] At the SFIO congress at Amiens in January 1914, the delegates enthusiastically applauded Hermann Müller, a Reichstag deputy and a member of the steering committee of the SPD, as he called for a Franco-German rapprochement. Louis Debreuilh, secretary of the Permanent Administrative Commission of the SFIO, affirmed that for the first time "cohesion, understanding, and concord between the two parties have ceased to be theoretical and have become practical and effective."[82]

The tenth congress of the Second International was scheduled for Vienna in August of 1914. It was planned that this congress take up again the debate over the general strike to prevent war;[83] and in order to decide the French position on this question, the twelfth national congress of the SFIO met at Paris on July 15, 1914. There, after lengthy debate, the delegates voted approval of the general strike as a legitimate method to prevent war.[84]

Jaurès, especially, remained convinced that the French and German socialists could prevent their respective governments from plunging Europe into war. His confidence in the pacifist sentiment of his German colleagues never wavered. Two months before the French socialists gathered at Paris, he assured a friend that "four million German socialists will rise like one man and execute the Kaiser if he wants to start a war."[85]

The greatest challenge to French socialist pacifism before the war was the three-year law of 1913. Introduced in March of that year during the ministry of Louis Barthou, the proposal for the three-year law followed Germany's increase of her standing army to 850,000 in February. With an active land force of only 480,000 and a reserve army of 375,000, France was compelled to follow suit. But the nation, suffering from a declining birthrate, was unable to call up more men. The three-year law proposed to solve this problem by increasing the term of military service from two to three years, thus narrowing the numerical gap between the French and German armies.

In order to understand the determined campaign waged against this measure by the parliamentary socialists, who had already committed themselves to national defense, it is necessary to review their historic animosity to large standing armies. The pre-1905 socialists, as indicated earlier, persistently denounced professional standing armies and pleaded for the creation of a citizen army to be used only in case of invasion. After 1905 the idea of a citizen army remained a fundamental tenet in the socialist philosophy of military organization. Socialist speakers in the Chamber repeatedly emphasized this theme.[86] In October 1907 the party presented an Order of the Day calling for "an exclusively defensive foreign policy and the transformation of the permanent army into a national militia."[87] In June 1910 Albert Thomas read to the Chamber a declaration of the SFIO urging the transformation of the professional army into a national militia as "a prelude to progressive and simultaneous disarmament."[88]

Jaurès, strongly convinced that only a great body of armed citizens could successfully defend the nation, began in early 1910 to gather background material for a work that would outline his views on national defense and military organization. For months he perused works on military science in the Bibliothèque Nationale, especially those of General Ferdinand Foch;

and he spent hours in conversation with a brilliant young military theorist, Captain Henry Gérard. Jaurès's study only buttressed his idea that defensive tactics alone could ward off a German onslaught, as opposed to the fanatic belief of the professionals in "the offensive." In 1911 Jaurès published the results of his study in his book *L'Armée nouvelle*, in which he argued that a massive body of armed citizens could bear the brunt of a crushing German offensive, slowly withdraw while attacking enemy flanks and supply lines, and eventually drive out the invader.[89] A citizen army would provide for effective national defense, but it would be incapable of waging an aggressive war; thus, a citizen army would remove one of the chief causes of war, while assuring "the protection of national independence and the free evolution of social justice."[90]

A few months before actual publication of *L'Armée nouvelle*, Jaurès transformed his ideas into a bill, which he submitted to the Chamber of Deputies on November 14, 1910. Its most important article called for the reduction of active military service to six months and for military instruction and reserve training until the age of thirty-four, including training exercises at the military post nearest the soldier's home.[91] The measure was sent to the Commission of the Army; but despite Jaurès's skillful defense of its provisions before that group, which was amazed at his technical competence,[92] it failed to pass. Most biographies of Jaurès erroneously state that Jaurès's bill thus failed to reach the floor of the Chamber. While it is true that this particular bill failed to pass the Commission of the Army, its provisions came before the Chamber twice—the first time in the form of a "counter-project," defeated during a heated debate over reorganization of the infantry on December 9, 1912,[93] the second time in a similar manner during the debate over the three-year law.

The parliamentary socialists decided with Jaurès that the three-year proposal was the very antithesis of their concept of the army as a truly popular institution. They saw the proposal as a negation of their hopes to democratize military life, and they recognized an increase in armaments as a challenge to the pacifist policies they had advocated for ten years. On March 3, 1913, during a speech on laic schools, Jaurès drew thunderous applause from the Extreme Left when he digressed momentarily to warn that the socialists would fight "this inane and perilous law" with all their strength.[94] When Eugène Etienne, minister of war in Barthou's cabinet, introduced the law three days later, the socialist protest was so noisy that he was unable to read the first paragraph. Vaillant referred to the measure as "this mortal coup to the Republic," and Jaurès termed it "a crime and a folly."[95]

As the newspapers supporting the three-year law began their campaign, especially *Le Temps* and *Matin,* Jaurès, Thomas, Allard, and Sembat countered with their own crusade in the pages of *Humanité.* Vigorous articles against the measure appeared each day throughout March, April, May, and June.[96] On March 1 the French and German socialists issued a joint manifesto protesting the increases in the armies of both countries.[97] In a party caucus on March 7 Guesde and Vaillant formulated a resolution condemning the three-year law and demanding that France open negotiations with Germany to reduce armaments.[98] A few days later *Humanité* announced a public petition against the three-year law, which by July 7 had acquired 738,269 signatures.[99]

The socialists carried their campaign against the three-year law to their party congress at Brest on March 23, 24, and 25. Vaillant warned that passage of the measure would stir chauvinistic passions in France and Germany. Pressensé (who died in February of the next year) delivered one of the most eloquent speeches of his career in which he predicted that the "imbecilic" three-year law would lead to war. Compère-Morel castigated the three-year law as a product of "chauvinistic and military reaction" and proposed a resolution, which was adopted unanimously, declaring that the establishment of a national militia, maintenance of the two-year law, international arbitration, and a Franco-German rapprochement were the only roads to peace.[100]

The debate at Brest stimulated the socialists to even greater resistance, and the various federations of the party organized "peace demonstrations" throughout France.[101] The largest of these was staged at Pré-Saint-Gervais on May 25. At this afternoon rally, organized by the SFIO and the General Confederation of Labor, Jaurès assailed the three-year law before a crowd of over 150,000, one of the high points in the history of the pre-1914 French socialist movement.[102]

Jaurès realized that defeat of the three-year law could not be achieved through socialist efforts alone. He therefore turned to the leader of the Radical-Socialists, Joseph Caillaux, whose peace efforts during the second Moroccan crisis had earned socialist respect.[103] Jaurès had great confidence in Caillaux's statesmanship and had once remarked to the German Liberal deputy Conrad Haussmann that Caillaux was "one of the most capable men in France. He is not only capable, but he is also a man of decisive will and character. That is why he is so violently attacked."[104] Thus, one evening in early June of 1913, Jaurès dined with Caillaux at the home of Charles Paix-Séailles, a friend of the ex-premier. In his memoirs Caillaux tells us that "an agreement was concluded between us. . . . It was agreed that we would make a great effort against the three-year law, and that if we were defeated we would demand that the income tax pay for the extra year of service."[105] But in his opposition to the three-year law, Caillaux, as events would show, could not speak for all of his party.

Debate on the three-year proposal was begun on June 2 and lasted for seven intensive weeks. On June 3 Joseph Reinach put forth the case for the bill in a three-hour speech that drew continued attacks from socialists such as Paul Aubriot (Seine), Albert Bedouce (Haute-Garonne), Pierre Roblin (Nièvre), Jean Colly, Raffin Dugens, and Vaillant.[106] Two weeks later Albert Thomas delivered the first of another series of socialist assaults against the measure. Thomas argued that the problem of the law was not strictly military. It would drain 200,000 more young men from their jobs, thus inflicting serious damage on the nation's industry and agriculture. In addition, maintaining soldiers for an extra year of duty would require enormous sums that ought to be used for social legislation. Thomas also questioned the usefulness of the additional men in repulsing a German attack, and he reiterated the ideas set down by Jaurès in *L'Armée nouvelle.*[107]

Jean Colly, a former mechanic elected deputy for the Seine in 1910, next defended the socialists against the charge that their opposition to the bill was exposing the nation to defeat. He contended that a sincere application of the two-year law, which was the first step toward a national militia, was adequate for national defense.[108] Vaillant, confident of public sympathy for the socialist position (as evidenced by the almost 800,000 signatures to the socialist petition against the three-year law), suggested that the conflict be resolved by referendum. When Premier Barthou answered that such an act would be unconstitutional, Vaillant rejoined that the premier feared to consult the nation because he knew that it would repudiate the irresponsible foreign policy that had necessitated the proposed three-year law. Despite the support of a number of Radical-Socialists, Vaillant's motion failed by a vote of 410 to 159.[109]

The following day Vaillant presented a "counter-project" which called for a national militia similar to the Swiss Federal Army. This time only seventy-one members supported him,[110] thus revealing that the Radicals who opposed the three-year law were still unwilling to go to the socialist extreme of a citizen army. Jaurès immediately presented another motion providing

37

for eighteen months of active duty followed by two weeks of intensive military training each year.[111] The next day he defended this proposal in a speech based primarily on the ideas in *L'Armée nouvelle*,[112] but two days later it was defeated by a vote of 496 to 77.[113]

The socialists entertained no expectation of victory. These counterproposals were designed to gain time to mobilize public opinion against the three-year law and to persuade the undecided Radicals to join their cause. Thus, day after day throughout most of June 1913, various socialist deputies presented an endless succession of proposals constituting variations on the themes of Vaillant and Jaurès.[114] By the end of the month they recognized that only a miracle could prevent passage of the three-year measure. The impending victory of its proponents symbolized to the socialists the triumph of reaction and militarism, and they viewed this triumph with great bitterness. On June 26 Vaillant and Thomas charged that the three-year law was the fulfillment of a promise made in 1912 by President Poincaré, at that time premier, to Russian Minister Isvolsky.[115] In a turbulent session on July 4 the socialists engaged in violent verbal duels with members of the Right and Center. They cheered Sixte Quenin, socialist deputy for Bouches-du-Rhône, as he attacked Minister of War Eugène Etienne from the tribune, describing him as one of the chief chauvinists responsible for Franco-German tensions.[116] Five days later Lucien Voilin (Seine), Alexander Bracke (Seine), Jaurès, and Colly argued against cloture of debate and protested that the three-year law discriminated against the poor, who needed the labor of their sons at home.[117]

On July 18 Caillaux, faithful to his promise to Jaurès, dramatically intervened to prevent passage of the three-year law. His intervention accomplished little. The next day the Chamber passed the three-year law by a vote of 358 to 204. The socialists voted unanimously against it. Of the 133 Radical-

Socialists, 86 voted against and 47 for. Only 19 Radicals joined Caillaux against the bill, while 85 followed the Radical Premier Barthou. After the vote Henri de La Porte, socialist deputy for Deux-Sèvres, read a declaration of the SFIO stating that passage of the three-year law was indicative of the growing strength of reaction. The measure did not insure, but compromised, national defense. This "bastard and contradictory" law meant military disorganization, financial ruin, and national weakness; and the French socialists would fight for its repeal while combating the reactionary presidency of Raymond Poincaré.[118]

The question of the repeal of the three-year law dominated French politics until the crisis of July 1914. In October 1913 the Radicals and Radical-Socialists gathered at Pau, where the revived left wing of the party, arguing that Radicalism had gradually fallen to pieces under Briand, Poincaré, and Barthou, demanded immediate reforms. Painfully aware of the truth of these charges and conscious, too, of the advantage of collaborating with the Extreme Left during the coming legislative elections, the delegates capitulated to the demand for a left-wing program, elected Caillaux their president, and formally declared their opposition to the three-year law.[119]

The following January the socialists assembled at Amiens for their eleventh national congress. The delegates decided that in the coming elections of April and May the party would support on the second ballot all candidates favoring repeal of the three-year law.[120] This decision, which was essentially a call for the reconstitution of the *Bloc des Gauches*, was contrary to the Rheims-Dresden Resolution of 1904. Yet the socialists saw in the increase of the size of the army a grave threat to peace, and they felt that practical considerations for peace overruled any doctrinaire notions of revolutionary purity.

The socialist campaign for peace had appealed to a large segment of the electorate, and in the legislative elections of 1914 the socialists experienced their greatest victory to date. They garnered 1,398,771 votes plus 34 additional seats in the Chamber, bringing the total of socialist deputies to 101. The Radicals and Radical-Socialists maintained their preponderance in the Chamber with 228 deputies, and it appeared that a Caillaux-Jaurès coalition was a distinct possibility.[121]

What might have happened at this point if the war had not intervened is a subject of interesting speculation. Both Caillaux and his friend Paix-Séailles relate that shortly after the elections Jaurès and Caillaux discussed the formation of a new ministry. Caillaux proposed the creation of "a grand ministry of the left that can reconcile Europe." Such a ministry, he said, would require parliamentary and governmental collaboration of Radicals and socialists. In return for such support, Caillaux promised Jaurès the Ministry of Foreign Affairs. Jaurès objected that this would be contrary to the Rheims-Dresden Resolution, but he added that "given the imminent gravity of the situation, it might be necessary to discard the scholasticism of the party."[122]

Jaurès's apparent willingness to join a bourgeois ministry in order to aid the cause of peace casts a revealing light on the order of values he embraced. Jaurès, and doubtlessly not he alone, was willing to risk a repetition of the party crises of 1899 and 1904 in order to prevent a Franco-German war. A Caillaux-Jaurès ministry, combining the idealism and vision of the great socialist tribune with the pragmatism and hard sense of the Radical financial wizard, would have been an interesting experiment in a European system of diplomacy that stagnated from lack of able and imaginative men.

But Leftist hopes had not counted on the stubborn will of President Poincaré, who was determined to prevent repeal of the three-year law. On June 6 the Caillaux-Jaurès faction forced the resignation of Gaston Doumergue, then in his sixth month as president of the Council. Poincaré turned to the onetime socialist René Viviani, who, though he had not supported the three-year law, promised Poincaré that he would enforce it. But Viviani was unable to form a ministry. Stubbornly refusing to surrender to Caillaux, Poincaré then selected the aged Alexander Ribot, a staunch supporter of the three-year law; but he, too, was rebuffed by the Chamber on June 12. The next day Poincaré again consulted with Viviani, who was able this time to form a ministry, which he presented to the parliament on June 17. Seeking to direct the attention of the Left away from the three-year law, Viviani strongly emphasized his support of the income tax; and the Radicals, wishing to end the ministerial crisis, then in its third week, finally gave him their votes, while the socialists abstained.[123] This turn of events virtually eliminated the possibility of a Caillaux-Jaurès ministry.

French socialist attitudes toward national defense from 1904 to 1914 reveal a basic ambiguity resulting from the attempt to reconcile Marxian internationalism with patriotism. Like good Marxists, the French socialists denounced the capitalist governments that would throw the workers into war, and they struggled against the unhealthy nationalism that threatened the unstable peace. But if one defines Marxian internationalism as the idea of a proletariat without country, loyal to class rather than to nation-state, then the French socialists were not Marxists. They were Frenchmen first and socialists second. They insisted on the coexistence of patriotism and internationalism. They sought peace, but they were ready to support France in a just and defensive war. They failed to foresee that any war involving France would be presented to the nation as a just and defensive response to an unprovoked attack.

Despite this ambiguity, the French socialists were essentially pacifist. They never abandoned the search for an unarmed world. The yearly vote against the budget was not a matter of show; it was a fundamental tenet of the pact of unity, and the bitterness with which the socialists denounced military expenditures was a measure of their earnestness. Their opposition to increased armaments, their plan for a citizen army for defense only, and their pleas in the Chamber, in the press, and at their party congresses for international arbitration, disarmament, and Franco-German reconciliation are marks of the sincerity with which they hoped for an age of peace.

SOCIALISM AND CZARISM:

AN UNWANTED ALLIANCE AND

A REVOLUTION THAT FAILED

The French socialists abhorred the "unnatural union" of Czarist Russia with Republican France from the very moment of its conclusion. They detested the autocracy of Czarism and feared that the secret clauses of the Franco-Russian Alliance, which were the antithesis of the socialist concept of agreements openly arrived at, might involve France in a faraway war in which it had no interest.[1] Guesde expressed these sentiments in 1893 when he stated that "we do not want a war which . . . would only bring upon the weakened west the yoke of Asiatic barbarianism represented by Russian Czarism."[2] Two years earlier, at the Second International congress at Brussels (1891),

Vaillant declared that while he was "no admirer of the Triple Alliance," it at least served as a restraint upon the French chauvinism which had resulted in a humiliating union with Czarism.[3] The hostility of the French socialists toward Czarism increased in 1896 because French inaction during the Armenian massacres convinced the socialists that their country had capitulated to Russian demands to stay out of these areas.[4] In 1897 Millerand attacked the secrecy of the Franco-Russian Alliance in the Chamber of Deputies, demanding that its terms be made known to the parliament.[5]

The French socialists repeatedly stressed their hostility to Czarism and the Franco-Russian Alliance in their reactions to developments within Russia between 1904 and 1914. The major issues upon which they based their anti-Czarist campaign included their demands for French neutrality during the Russo-Japanese War, their sympathy for the revolutionary movement in Russia between 1904 and 1907, their protests against loans to Russia that strengthened Czarist resistance to this movement, and their charges that Nicholas II was using France to further his own interests—interests which, the socialists claimed, would ultimately involve France in war.

By February of 1904 rivalry in the Far East had touched off a deadly struggle between Russia and Japan. A few days after the outbreak of war, Jaurès wrote in the *Dépêche de Toulouse*: "If we should ever be led by secret commitments to the brink of war, the country will never forgive those who, for a decade, have smothered in a cloud of patriotism all those questions that the socialists have tried to raise."[6] As the struggle continued, the extent of Russian weakness was unveiled by repeated defeats, despite attempts of the French press to minimize the disasters.[7] Jaurès was not deceived. He wrote in *Humanité* on January 25, 1905, that "[it] is Czardom, the regime of autocracy, waste, corruption, and stupidity, which has unleashed ruinous wars and exhausted the resources of a great people."[8]

44

The alliance system placed France in a peculiar position after the outbreak of the Russo-Japanese War. As a result of the Anglo-French entente of April 8, 1904, France was now allied to England, which was the ally of Japan, which was the enemy of Russia, which was the major ally of France. Amidst this confusion of alliances it was difficult for France to aid its faltering ally without abandoning its neutrality and without offending Great Britain. France allowed the Russian fleet to refuel and to carry out intensive training programs at the French possessions of Nossi-Be (Madagascar) and Kamranh (Cochin-China). Japan protested this breach of neutrality, and the British House of Commons took note of the prolonged stay of Russian ships in French harbors.[9] The danger of British entry into the Russo-Japanese War (which probably would have been followed by French entry on the opposing side) was illustrated on October 21-22, 1904, when the Russian Baltic Fleet opened fire on some British trawlers off Dogger Bank. Fortunately for Britain, France, and Russia, war was avoided by the frantic efforts of French diplomats.[10]

The French parliamentary socialists feared French involvement. On November 10, 1904, Pressensé reminded the government of its obligations of neutrality. Referring to the war as a "barbaric, bloody conflict, offering victims upon the altar of the god of militarism," he urged French and British diplomatic intervention to bring it to a close.[11] On April 19, 1905, Victor Dejeante, socialist deputy for the Seine, affirmed that the parliamentary socialists would not rest until the government was neutral in fact as well as in name.[12] The following month Vaillant again pleaded for neutrality, and Pressensé warned that the visits of Russian ships to French harbors continued to increase British resentment.[13]

The fact that France did not formally aid its impotent ally failed to diminish socialist hatred for the alliance and Czarism. When, as a result of increasing dissatisfaction with the bungling

Czarist government, revolution broke out in Russia in November 1904, the French socialists believed that Czarist autocracy had seen its last days and that the Russian people were about to achieve freedom. They viewed the revolution as "our revolution and the prologue of a great revolution that will break the chains of the universal proletariat."[14] Guesde, especially, felt that the Russian revolution confirmed that war in the capitalist order was not only inevitable but often desirable as a means of bringing about social revolution.[15]

But French socialist hopes for the triumph of the revolutionary movement were soon disappointed. On January 22, 1905, unarmed workers were shot down in front of the Winter Palace in St. Petersburg. On the day following the tragedy of "Red Sunday" (a term coined by Jaurès),[16] the socialist leader wrote that "the Czar and the regime he represents are outlaws in human society."[17] Two days after the St. Petersburg massacre the socialists in the Chamber greeted Premier Maurice Rouvier's reference to "our cherished alliance" with shouts of "Down with the assassins! Down with the Czar!" Maurice Allard declared that he was amazed to hear a minister speak before a French parliament of an alliance with "a government of assassins." Foreign Minister Thèophile Delcassé, protesting the language of the socialists, was cut short by the socialist deputies Adrien Meslier, Jules Coutant, and Gustave Rouanet, who bitterly condemned the Czarist government. Delcassé meekly replied that the socialists should not be the judges. Jaurès retorted that the foreign minister was advocating the slaughter of a people.[18]

The next day the socialists organized a demonstration of six thousand people in Paris to protest the murder of the workers, and on February 18 and 19 the socialists organized twenty-one demonstrations throughout France "to affirm the solidarity of the French working class with the heroic combatants of Russian liberty."[19] The following October, at their national party

46

congress at Chalon-sur-Saône, the socialist delegates passed a similar resolution.[20]

The massacre of the St. Petersburg workers only increased agitation within Russia. The devastating effects of the war with Japan, which ended with Russia's defeat, created even more discontent. Strikes and peasant disturbances brought the nation's life to a virtual halt, and in the fall of 1905 Czar Nicholas II was compelled to issue his "October Manifesto," granting Russia a constitution.[21]

Although the manifesto included provisions for the establishment of a representative assembly, the 1905 revolution was arrested before it had freed the Russian people. Almost as soon as it was organized, the impotence of the Duma, Russia's first representative assembly in modern times, was revealed. Its powers were too slight to challenge Nicholas, whose financial independence of this advisory and legislative body was partially assured by a French loan in January 1906.[22] Without ministerial responsibility the Duma was unable to enforce its agrarian reform decree in the summer of that year. On July 9, 1906, the czar charged that the Duma had exceeded its powers and dissolved it. Disorder again plagued the country; and Peter Stolypin, the energetic minister of the interior, soon to become prime minister, established military courts in order to mete out quick punishment to rebellious subjects. Any semblance of civil liberty was abolished as Stolypin's courts tried hundreds of people between September 1906 and April 1907. At Stolypin's suggestion, however, Nicholas ordered elections for a new Duma in February 1907. It, too, was condemned to the fate of the first. Conflict arose when it rejected Stolypin's agrarian reforms. In June 1907 Nicholas dissolved the second Duma, after accusing the Social Democrats of plotting against his life. The czar delivered the final blow to the 1905 revolution when he altered the electoral law for the third Duma, which lasted until 1912, by increasing decisively the representation of large landowners.

The French socialists were incensed by the czar's brutal suppression of political and civil liberties. At the same time, they vented their indignation on the French government, delivering ferocious attacks on French investment in Russia, including loans to the Czarist government. They believed that these funds strengthened the czar's struggle against the revolutionary movement, and they argued that the incessant drain on French finances weakened social legislation at home. On April 12, 1906, Vaillant announced to the Chamber that he and his colleagues felt that the approval of new loans to the czar was a betrayal of the Russian people. The old Communard pointed out that the decayed Russian Empire was rapidly marching toward an inevitable financial collapse. He noted that the revolutionary parties in Russia had declared their refusal to recognize the obligations implicit in these loans. Vaillant concluded that France should at least wait until the Duma had assembled before approving new loans.[23]

In February of the next year the parliamentary socialists delivered a sharp attack against the sale of Russian securities in France. They charged that a consortium of French financial interests had lured Frenchmen into buying Russian securities on the pretext of developing Russia's industrial resources. Gustave Rouanet, Adrien Meslier, Albert Willm, and Jaurès termed these "abusive, illegal stock exchange maneuvers" merely loans in disguise, intended to strengthen Nicholas II against the revolutionary movement. Rouanet complained that French citizens were losing hundreds of millions of francs. Even the French bourgeoisie had been betrayed, Vaillant charged; and he appealed to Joseph Caillaux, at that time minister of finance in Clemenceau's government, to uphold the honor and interests of France by preventing the sending of French silver to the treasury of an autocrat. Adrien Meslier argued that the drain of silver increased poverty at home; Russia, he said, needed liberty rather than gold. Foreign Minister Stéphen Pichon protested the socialist language. Vaillant retorted that his party spoke in the name of the Russian people; and Jules Coutant added that the French socialists regarded the Russian people as their friends, who had been trampled under the heel of "that assassin, the Czar." Coutant was called to order, and Pichon again reprimanded the socialists for vilifying France's ally.[24]

The next day Jaurès and Albert Willm, who was a lawyer and part-time journalist for the newspaper *Socialiste* as well as deputy for the Seine, continued the attack. In their struggle to help the Russian people achieve freedom, Willm contended, the French socialists were "the faithful guardians of our revolutionary tradition." This sentiment was not only the feeling of socialists, he went on, but also that of many Liberals, Republicans, Democrats, Radicals, and Christian Socialists. But the reactionary Czarist government had destroyed any hope of achieving that freedom through peaceful constitutional and social reform. "Witness the dissolution of the first Duma," he said, "and the twisted electoral law of the second and the mass arrests among the electors." He noted that even the Cadet party, neither socialist nor revolutionary, had been severely restricted in its campaign activities of December 1906 in order to assure a governmental majority in the second Duma.

Like Rouanet the previous day, Willm emphasized that Russia was in no condition to repay French loans. Jules Delafosse, Rightist deputy for Calvados, protested that the socialists had no right to judge the internal affairs of foreign governments; but Victor Dejeante and Marcel Sembat rejoined that loans to the czar jeopardized French interests and that the socialists were thus compelled to speak their convictions.[25] Jaurès added that French loans and investments furnished arms against the Russian people; thus, he reasoned, the financial syndicates, backed by the French government, bore the real guilt for meddling in the internal affairs of other countries.[26] But the socialist protests did not avail, and Pichon's firm defense of the alliance evoked Russian Foreign Minister Alexander Isvolsky's thanks for the "categorical language" with which he had answered socialist protests.[27]

Such failures did not still the socialists' attacks. Jean Longuet, grandson of Karl Marx and nephew of Paul Lafargue, denounced the Clemenceau government for furnishing guns and ammunition to "the assassins who run the Russian government."[28] Gustave Rouanet wrote a series of articles in *Humanité* in which he condemned the Russian loans.[29] In the same newspaper the czar was satirized in political cartoons. One of these, appearing on November 16, 1907, pictured Nicholas II speaking to members of the Duma who were hanging from the rafters of a meeting hall: "Members of the second Duma, I welcome you. Your election is proof of our country's progress."[30] Socialist editorialists, such as Léon Rémy, bitterly indicted the czar's reactionary court;[31] and Jaurès wrote prophetically, after the failure of the second Duma, that the Russian working class would never achieve political liberty except through violence.[32]

After the dissolution of the second Duma the French parliamentary socialists issued a manifesto expressing solidarity with the persecuted Cadets, Social Democrats, and Social Revolutionaries. The manifesto declared that "constitutional government in Russia is only a hypocritical fiction" and acknowledged that the Russian people were not responsible for repaying French loans made to the czar.[33] In the Chamber, Vaillant fiercely attacked Stolypin for his part in the court-martial of leading members of the Duma. According to Vaillant, the Russian prime minister had been responsible for 1,292 executions in 1906, 1,692 in 1907, 767 in the first three months of 1908, and 134 in April 1908.[34]

The state visit of French President Armand Fallières to Russia in July 1908 provoked the socialists to even more violent attacks against loans to the czar. The visit (which was to carry the president to Norway, Denmark, Sweden, and Russia) was assailed by a unanimous resolution of the National Council of the SFIO proposed by Jean Longuet on June 14.[35] In the Chamber on June 29 Vaillant presented an amendment, signed by all fifty-four socialists, reducing by 50,000 francs an appropriation of 400,000 francs to finance Fallières's visit, attempting thus to prevent the inclusion of Russia in the president's schedule. Vaillant charged that the sole purpose of the trip was to arrange new loans: "Once again you wish to drain the public fortune of France . . . [and] to extend to the Czar the instrument with which to oppose the Russian people, who have suffered too long from hunger, fear, and political intimidation." Both Pichon and Clemenceau denied the accusation; and the Chamber, ignoring castigations of Clemenceau by Allard and Dejeante, approved credits for the voyage over the socialist opposition.[36]

Outside the Chamber the socialists continued their denunciation of the state visit. The next day the editorialist Pierre Bertrand denounced in *Humanité* those deputies who had voted credits for the voyage.[37] Marcel Sembat, also writing in *Humanité*, charged the czar with crimes and assassinations;[38] and Elysée Lasalle, deputy for Ardennes, praised the Russian people for their heroic struggle against a tyrant supported by an insensitive French government.[39] On July 3 the socialist Federation of the Seine (the second largest in the SFIO) held a protest rally at Paris. The Social Revolutionary I. A. Rubanovitch, Russian delegate to the International Socialist Bureau, and the French deputies Sembat, Rouanet, Vaillant, Allard, André Dubois (Seine), and Henri Ghesquière (Nord) attacked Russian despotism and praised the resistance of the Russian people.[40] Four days later the parliamentary socialists and the twenty-two members of the Permanent Administrative Commission published a manifesto to the workers of France condemning the president's trip, which "placed at the disposition of a tyrant at war against his own people the gold, influence, and credit of the French Republic."[41] Throughout the summer of 1908[42] the socialists pressed their anti-Czarist campaign; and at their congress at Toulouse in October, the delegates again criticized Fallières's visit to Russia as dishonoring the Republic.[43]

The negative attitude of the French socialists toward the Franco-Russian Alliance was counterbalanced by their proposals for a different kind of alliance system. During the debates over ratification of the Anglo-French entente of 1904,[44] the parliamentary socialists stressed the need for a rapprochement between the western democracies—Italy, France, and England. Jaurès referred to the Triple Alliance as "a necessary counterweight against our chauvinism and Franco-Russian fantasies" and expressed his belief that "one of the forces of humane action in Europe is the recent rapprochement of the three great countries of liberty, democracy, and representative government—Italy, France, and England."[45] Jaurès drew applause from the Extreme Left when he told the Chamber, on November 7, 1904, that a reconciliation of the western democracies was a step toward universal peace.[46] Three days later Pressensé suggested that a concrete alliance with England was the best guarantee for preventing French isolation in Europe,[47] and Jaurès again argued that the Franco-Russian Alliance did not preclude French alliances with other nations.[48] In the years following the first Moroccan crisis the socialists began to include Germany in this western alliance, urging the creation of an "Anglo-French-German entente."[49]

French socialist opposition to the Franco-Russian Alliance and Czarist imperialism remained an essential part of socialist foreign policy attitudes to 1914. The French socialists condemned the Anglo-Russian treaty of 1907 that had "partitioned and devoured Persia,"[50] and they attacked Russian imperialism in that Moslem kingdom torn by social and political disturbances.[51] They denounced Isvolsky's role in the Austrian annexation of Bosnia and Herzegovina in 1908;[52] and the next year

Pressensé charged that French loans to Imperial Russia had committed the nation to support Czarist imperialism in the Balkans, which would eventually drag France into war.[53] Jaurès noted in the Chamber on January 12, 1911, that Russia had recently granted to Germany a free hand in the building of the Bagdad Railway in return for a free hand in Persia. Thus, he added sarcastically, while France faithfully loaned money to the czar, Russia returned the favor by making secret agreements with the Germans in order to further Czarist imperialism.[54] The next day Jaurès emphasized that France was a Great Power seeking peace and must not allow itself to be used by the czar to carry out his ambition.[55]

The following December, Sembat argued that the Franco-Russian Alliance must not limit France's freedom to act in the best interests of peace. The French socialists, he said, saw the alliance as the major obstacle to Franco-German reconciliation; and they hoped, despite the failure of the democratic movement in Russia, that the alliance would eventually be transformed into an instrument of peace.[56] Jaurès reiterated Sembat's idea when the government requested funds for the voyage of President Poincaré and Premier Viviani to St. Petersburg shortly after Ferdinand's assassination at Sarajevo. The socialists refused to approve these funds and charged that the two heads of state were traveling to the Russian capital to arrange new loans.[57] A few hours before his own assassination on July 31, 1914, Jaurès led a socialist delegation to plead with Abel Ferry, under-secretary of state, for a last effort for peace. Summing up the anti-Czarist sentiments expressed so long by the socialists, he told Ferry, "You are all the victims of Isvolsky and Russian intrigue; we are going to denounce all of you light-headed ministers, even should we be shot."[58]

The French socialist anti-Czarist agitation between 1904 and 1914, while producing few tangible results, again reveals the extent to which the socialists considered peace the supreme goal of their foreign policy. They believed that if the revolutionary movement in Russia had succeeded, the Franco-Russian Alliance could have been transformed into an instrument of peace; but they foresaw, though their warnings went unheeded, that unconditional French support of an alliance with a reactionary czar could only lead France into a war it did not want. At the same time, they realized that the failure of the Duma indicated that more violent measures would be necessary to achieve freedom in Russia; and their expressions of sympathy for the struggling Russian revolutionary movement were in accordance with those foreign policy principles that Jaurès had defined to the Chamber on December 8, 1905: hatred of tyranny, belief in democracy and social justice, and sympathy for working-class movements in other countries.

THE ROAD TO MOROCCO

Between 1904 and 1914 French socialist views on colonialism were centered almost exclusively around the problems arising from the French conquest of Morocco. With the signing of the Entente Cordiale in April 1904, France gained British approval to penetrate this last area in North Africa open to colonization. Germany, however, would not be denied its share of the spoils; and in 1905, 1908, and 1911 Franco-German confrontations in Morocco threatened Europe with the war that the French socialists were desperately trying to avoid.

The agreement with England represented an important achievement for French Foreign Minister Thèophile Delcassé, whose policies sought to consolidate the French holdings in North Africa and to strengthen the French position in Europe.[1] During the debates over ratification from November 3 to 10, 1904, the socialists reflected the favorable sentiment throughout both France and England[2] by their enthusiastic approval of Delcassé's efforts. Pressensé and Jaurès spoke for the party, supporting the agreement with the reservation that the accord must not become a stepping-stone to a more vigorous colonial policy. Socialist policy toward Morocco, they said, was one of "peaceful penetration," not annexation or invasion by "military adventurers filled with nationalist poison." The socialists defined peaceful penetration as a humanitarian program based upon the introduction of European culture, agricultural and industrial improvements, and the building of schools, hospitals, and roads.

Jaurès, anticipating hostile repercussions in Berlin, stressed that the Anglo-French entente was not directed against Germany. It was "an instrument of peace that implied no secret distrust of others." Now that it was signed, France should work toward a reconciliation with Germany.[3] On November 10 the socialists voted unanimously for the agreement, which was ratified by a vote of 443 to 105.[4]

The socialists' acceptance of the policy of peaceful penetration was not a radical departure from their previous attitudes toward colonialism. Since the days of Jules Ferry, when France had entered the colonial race, they had approved humanitarian colonization, but had rejected "the methods of chauvinists and military adventurers."[5] In approving the accord, however, the socialists either ignored or failed to understand that for many French leaders it was indeed a stepping-stone to a more vigorous colonial policy. The conservative and highly influential *Journal des débats*, for example, wrote on November 18, 1904: "The important thing is that the agreement gives us the hope, almost the certainty, of hegemony in North Africa."[6]

56

The crisis that gripped Europe four months after the ratification of the Anglo-French accord painfully confirmed Jaurès's fear that Germany might interpret it as a hostile measure. Since the conclusion of the Franco-Russian Alliance, Germany had slowly become aware that the balance of power was shifting in France's favor. Russia's catastrophic defeat at the hands of Japan, along with the internal disorders that followed, temporarily eliminated that country as a Great Power and, accordingly, created a favorable moment to redress the balance in Germany's favor. Chancellor Bernhard von Bülow and Kaiser Wilhelm II thus gave their support to Friedrich von Holstein, the head of the political section of the Foreign Office, who hoped to exploit the Moroccan imbroglio to win a diplomatic victory.

The opportunity for German intervention came in early 1905 when a French mission to Fez attempted to conclude an agreement with the Moroccan sultan whereby France would gain financial and military control. On March 31, 1905, Wilhelm II, sword dangling from his side, landed at Tangier and dramatically announced Germany's intention to prevent the establishment of a French protectorate. Germany then proposed an international conference to settle the Moroccan dispute, wrongly believing that a showdown would expose the superficiality of the Entente Cordiale, humiliate and again isolate France, and consequently raise Germany's prestige in Europe.[7]

This test of wills marks the beginning of a definite change in socialist attitudes toward French expansion in Morocco. At the signing of the Anglo-French accord the socialists had hoped that it would bring European civilization to "inferior" races. They now began to realize that peaceful penetration usually degenerated into military conquest. Furthermore, it became apparent to them that such conquest created dangerous international friction. Thus, socialist support for a presumable policy of peaceful, enlightened colonization gradually changed into anxiety and eventually became opposition.

On April 7 the socialists queried the government on the Moroccan situation and the state of Franco-German relations. Delcassé, announcing France's refusal to yield, insisted that Germany was bluffing and reminded his interrogators that he had upheld French interests and had formulated his policies with the consent of the nation and the parliament. Vaillant, Jaurès, Pressensé, and Sembat retorted that he had carried his expansionism too far and upbraided him for his refusal to negotiate. Vaillant declared that the socialists preferred insurrection at home to war over a colonial matter.[8]

As the crisis continued, socialist denunciations of Delcassé's refusal to negotiate became more virulent. On April 19 Jaurès accused the foreign minister of twisting the meaning of the Entente Cordiale by excluding Germany from his Moroccan plans. The socialist leader recalled that, on April 9 and 12 of the previous year, German Chancellor Bülow had spoken of the Anglo-French accord with sympathy before the Reichstag.[9] Jaurès claimed that in a personal conversation he himself had then urged Delcassé to use that rare moment of cordiality to effect a rapprochement with Germany. Instead, he complained, Delcassé had disregarded this advice, embarking on a course of "reckless and irresponsible diplomacy." He had mistakenly regarded Germany as a "negligible quantity"; and his interpretation of the entente with England had been "narrow, chauvinistic, and menacing," based upon a policy of "adventure, incoherence, and imprudence." Vaillant, Dejeante, and Pressensé voiced socialist support of Jaurès's ideas, criticizing Delcassé for his failure to understand German feelings of insecurity. Few of the deputies of the Left or Center attempted to answer the socialists, and even Premier Maurice Rouvier intimated that he favored a compromise settlement with Germany.[10]

Delcassé remained unmoved by socialist arguments or by his own party's dissension. His continued refusal to negotiate and his desire to contract a military alliance with England prompted these threatening words from Bülow on June 1: "We would have to make the only logical assumption possible if France . . . were to persist in Delcassé's policy of intimidation."[11] Socialist denunciation of these policies, though vigorous, contributed little to the subsequent fall of the powerful head of the Quai d'Orsay. Delcassé's overthrow was brought about by Rouvier, who understood that the France of 1905 was unprepared for war with Germany, despite the foreign minister's promise of British aid. On June 6 the Council of Ministers met at the Elysée and voted against Delcassé's proposal to seek a military alliance with England. He thereupon offered his resignation, and it was accepted.[12]

Germany, however, not satisfied with a diplomatic victory, insisted on an international conference. The French socialists favored this proposal, and they warmly applauded Rouvier's statement to the Chamber on July 11 that France was ready to attend a conference if certain principles were agreed on beforehand.[13] In the fall of 1905 a conference was scheduled for January 1906 at Algeciras, near Gibraltar.

The socialists were anxious for an amiable settlement. One month before the conference they warned that if the government should prove to be intransigent during the talks and seek to secure its own rights at the expense of others, "tragic consequences" would follow.[14] After the Powers had gathered at Algeciras on January 16, 1906, the socialists challenged the guarded silence of Rouvier (who had taken Delcassé's place at the Foreign Office) in regard to the proceedings. Jaurès, Vaillant, and Jules Coutant emphasized the socialist ideal of popular diplomacy, stressing that only the parliament and the people could safeguard the interests of France. Jaurès admitted that Germany had not always made the path to conciliation easy, but he warned against playing Germany's game of risking the foreign policy of the nation over "this miserable Moroccan quarrel."[15]

The Algeciras conference ended on April 7. Although the Powers agreed to preserve the territorial integrity of Morocco and to guarantee commercial equality, France gained control of the police force.[16] Germany had brought about what it feared most: a strengthening of the Entente Cordiale; closer relations between Russia, France, and England; and international approval of the French toehold in Morocco.[17] The French socialists were extremely pleased with the outcome. On April 12, when Léon Bourgeois, minister of foreign affairs in Ferdinand Sarrien's new government, reported on the results of Algeciras, Vaillant and Gustave Rouanet praised the settlement as a step toward universal peace.[18]

The government did not enjoy socialist support long. When riots broke out at Tangier the following September as a result of dissatisfaction with the sultan's rule, France sent three ships to that port city to protect French lives and property. The socialists challenged this move by the new government of Georges Clemenceau, arguing that it was the first step toward military penetration of the entire country.[19] Jaurès charged that the sending of ships would anger the sultan and provoke him into appealing to Germany, thus giving Germany the pretext to precipitate another crisis. Germany was distrustful and nervous, he explained, having never forgotten a past of weakness and division. French foreign policy should not tempt Germany to assert itself. Jaurès then proposed an amendment approving the Algeciras agreement but denouncing "any and every policy of adventure in Morocco." Although the Chamber rejected Jaurès's amendment, the socialists joined in a unanimous ratification of the settlement of Algeciras.[20]

Throughout the first Moroccan crisis the French socialists displayed a conciliatory attitude toward Germany, even at the risk of being termed unpatriotic.[21] Their actions, however, left them open to charges of inconsistency and irresponsibility. In approving the equivocal principle of peaceful penetration, they approved the risks of Delcassé's policies, among which provocation of Germany was the greatest. They insisted that Germany's position in Morocco be recognized; but they unanimously approved the victory at Algeciras, even though French gains and German losses might prove to be a source of future irritation. Whenever a showdown threatened, the socialists assumed none of the resultant responsibility and laid all the blame on the "incoherent and imprudent" policy of the foreign minister.

Socialist fear that the sending of French ships to Tangier in September 1906 would lead to further military penetration and more dangerous international difficulties was well-founded. The agreement of Algeciras was only one act in a long and bitter drama that dominated French foreign policy for the next five years. The Radical senator Stéphen Pichon, who was foreign minister for both Clemenceau and Briand from 1906 to 1911 (and who had served briefly as resident minister in Tunisia during the Combes era), placed little restraint on the colonialist deputies fully committed to expansion in North Africa[22] or on the permanent officials at the Quai d'Orsay who remained devoted to Delcassé's expansionist policy.[23]

The "Moroccan wasp's nest" did not remain quiet for long. On March 19, 1907, Dr. Emile Mauchamp, chief of the French medical dispensary in Marrakech, was assassinated by Arab bandits. Fear mounted among the European inhabitants; and on March 23 the French government, lacking confidence in the ability of Abdul Aziz, the Moroccan sultan, to maintain order, moved troops from Algeria under General Hubert Lyautey, who occupied the village of Oudja and the entire eastern district of Morocco.[24]

In the Chamber of Deputies the socialists, led by Vaillant, protested these military movements. They charged that the "colonial syndicate" had provoked the Moroccan disorders to furnish a pretext for the armed backing of the government, and they warned that Germany would hold France responsible for the arbitrary actions of its generals.[25] This "colonial syndicate" —which, according to the socialists, consisted of the colonialists at home and the French industrial interests in the Moroccan coastal cities—often felt the lash of socialist wrath because of its influence on French foreign policy and because of the socialists' well-founded suspicion that it advocated the ruthless exploitation of native labor.[26]

The incidents of the next few months drew France more deeply into the Moroccan maelstrom. On July 30 a mob attacked French workers attempting to lay a railroad across an old Arab cemetery in Casablanca. Nine Europeans were killed, and France felt that the offenders must be punished swiftly. The next day the government ordered the ship *Galilée* from Tangier to Casablanca, touching off riots in the city. When a small party attempted to go ashore, a struggle broke out with a group of natives at the gates, causing the nervous commander of the *Galilée* to bombard the city. Six days later more ships arrived. A French force of 4,500 under General Drude occupied Casablanca and charged the cost of the expedition to the already impecunious sultan. In August the German-backed Mulay Hafid, half brother of the sultan and governor of the Marrakech district, who appealed to many Moroccans as the only man capable of saving the country from foreign domination, revolted against his helpless brother and proclaimed himself sultan at Marrakech. France thereupon threw its support behind Abdul Aziz. Morocco, torn between two rival sultans, each backed by a major Power, was thus plunged into a state of near anarchy. This chaos invited further French intervention, especially after January 1908, when the rebellious brother was proclaimed sultan at the northern capital of Fez. The rumor that Mulay Hafid was preparing a holy war against foreigners bred terror among the European inhabitants; and by early February the daring General d'Amade had brought the entire Chaouya, the area around Casablanca, under French control.[27]

Throughout these events the French socialists maintained an unrelenting campaign against the extension of French control in Morocco. Fearing a Franco-German rupture and recognizing that increasing French intervention stirred Moroccan religious and national passions, they based this campaign upon the demand that France withdraw all military forces and declare strict neutrality in the Moroccan civil war. On August 11, 1907, at their party congress at Nancy, and during a demonstration at Paris the following October, they stressed these points, denouncing colonial "robbery" and "freebooting" and protesting against the "barbarity committed at Casablanca by the government of the former adversary of colonial policy."[28] In *Humanité*, Jaurès, Sembat, Allard, and Allemane persistently condemned the "colonial syndicate" and pleaded for Moroccan independence.[29] In the Chamber of Deputies throughout the fall of 1907 and the spring and summer of 1908, the socialists challenged the government no less than twelve times to adhere to the terms of Algeciras, criticizing the government for its failure to implement successfully the policy of peaceful penetration and charging that France would eventually march on Fez as a first step to making Morocco a protectorate. They also reiterated their warnings that Germany would not continue to tolerate France's flagrant violation of its commitments at Algeciras.

The French socialists' warnings fell on deaf ears, however; and their motions to end French military intervention and to maintain neutrality in the Moroccan civil war were invariably defeated.[30] Pichon allowed the generals even greater freedom, informing Saint-Aulaire, chargé d'affaires in Tangier, that France was to continue its "pacification" of Morocco and to "repulse all attacks wherever they come."[31] At the same time, France continued its support of the tottering Abdul Aziz, extending to him a loan through the Bank of France and recognizing him as the "only legal obstacle to the complete reign of anarchy in all the Moroccan Empire."[32]

By the end of the summer of 1908, despite French aid, Abdul Aziz had lost all authority in his empire. The new sultan, Mulay Hafid, had partially restored order; and by early fall France had recognized him. According to Jaurès, the Moroccan affair had now entered a new phase. Even though the restoration of order under the new sultan had supposedly eliminated the reason for military penetration, Jaurès predicted that France would continue to intervene and by doing so would turn the entire Moslem world against France.[33] This country, he lamented, had already lost the respect of the Moroccans. Inept diplomacy had led the nation to back a certain loser, and the new sultan now had just grievances against France. In addition, the triumph of the German-backed Mulay Hafid meant that "aristocratic, feudal, and militaristic" Germany had won the esteem of the Moroccans.[34]

This sophistic argument became academic in the face of a new Franco-German crisis in October 1908. Six deserters from the French Foreign Legion, three of them German, attempted with the aid of the German consul to reach a vessel in the harbor of Casablanca. French officials learned of the planned flight and reached the harbor in time to prevent it. When the consul tried to protect the deserters, the French officials threatened him with a gun and jailed his protégés. This incident contained all the elements of another major crisis. France claimed that desertion, regardless of the deserter's nationality, was a military crime. Germany claimed that service in a foreign army did not deprive an individual of his nationality and that the French officials were wrong to threaten a consul at the point of a gun.

The specter of a Franco-German war again haunted the socialists. On October 16, 1908, at their national party congress at Toulouse, they urged an immediate settlement and castigated Clemenceau and the Chamber of Deputies for giving the imperialists a "blank check" in Morocco.[35] At a socialist caucus on November 6 of the same year, Vaillant, Sembat, Willm, and

Varenne expressed hope that the Casablanca incident would not lead to war. They recalled socialist efforts to ease international tensions during the Fashoda crisis of 1898 and affirmed their determination to work for a Franco-German rapprochement.[36] Fortunately, both countries were anxious for a peaceful settlement and decided to submit the issue to the Hague Court, which ruled in favor of the French the following year.[37]

Socialist hopes for an end to Franco-German tensions in Morocco were soon realized, at least temporarily, by the Franco-German agreement of February 8, 1909. Economic considerations, rather than the socialist crusade for peace, produced the treaty. The Casablanca incident had impressed upon both the French and German governments that neither country could gain its share of Moroccan wealth without an amicable agreement. The disorders over the past four years had weakened French economic penetration and slowed the German port-improvement work at Tangier and Larache.[38] In the agreement of 1909, which formed the basis for Franco-German relations to 1911, Germany recognized France's "special interests" in Morocco and promised not to interfere with the maintenance of internal order; France, in turn, agreed to "maintain the integrity and independence of the Sherifian Empire" and promised not to hinder German commercial and industrial interests.[39]

Few socialists viewed this agreement with satisfaction. Jaurès hoped that the treaty would be the first step toward a rapprochement with Germany, but he feared that it might strengthen capitalist exploitation of the Moroccans.[40] Sembat had similar feelings,[41] and throughout 1909 and 1910 the parliamentary socialists continued to excoriate the government for its destruction of Moroccan independence.[42]

Meanwhile, the situation in Morocco deteriorated even further. France prolonged its occupation of Casablanca, the Chaouya, and the eastern district of the country. Germany failed to reap the commercial gains envisioned in the 1909 treaty,[43] and chronic disorder and financial insolvency undermined the authority of Mulay Hafid.

In January 1911 a native band, led by Zaer tribesmen of eastern Morocco, attacked French troops, killing five. Pichon demanded reparations, but the sultan was in no condition to pay. Pichon's successor, Jean Cruppi, selected as foreign minister when Ernest Monis formed his ministry on March 2, 1911, decided that tougher action was necessary. On March 14 he informed the chancelleries of Europe that he was ordering two battalions and two artillery divisions to Casablanca to occupy the city of Rabat, supply base for the Zaers.[44]

The same day that Cruppi informed Europe of these latest military movements, Emile Dumas, the new socialist deputy for the Cher, challenged the action; but his demand for debate was turned down.[45] Ten days later Jaurès pressed for debate again, claiming that internal disorders had continued in Morocco because the sultan's power had been undermined by constant French intervention. Jaurès pictured the Moroccan affair as a vicious circle. French presence provoked native rebellions, which France in turn used to extend its military control. Supported by the socialist deputies Adéodat Compère-Morel, Raffin Dugens, and Joseph Lagrosillière (Martinique), Jaurès urged that reason and conscience form the basis for French foreign policy rather than selfish interests. But the Chamber again expressed confidence in the Moroccan policy of the government by a vote of 365 to 74.[46]

By late April of 1911, when a revolt broke out at Fez, internal order in Morocco had almost vanished. Mulay Hafid requested French aid to restore order; and although the Chamber of Deputies was in Easter recess at the time, Cruppi ordered 25,000 men from Casablanca to Fez, which was occupied on May 21. On June 16 Jaurès, in the name of his party, protested the march on Fez, recalling that he had predicted this move in February 1908 when Clemenceau had only scoffed at his prediction. "But now we are in Fez," Jaurès accused, "and since the accession of the new Sultan our policy has been a continuous transgression of the treaty of Algeciras." France must therefore bear the responsibility for any German retaliation. Vaillant then submitted a motion, signed by all the socialists, demanding complete and immediate withdrawal of all French forces. The motion failed by a vote of 471 to 112.[47] Despite this failure, a number of Radicals and Radical-Socialists, as this last vote indicated, supported Vaillant's motion because they, too, disapproved of the French march on Fez and feared German retaliation.

Despite French assurances to Germany that the occupation of Fez was temporary, the retaliation of which Jaurès and Vaillant had warned was not long in coming. Germany believed, as in 1905, that the European situation demanded a redress of the balance of power. A. von Kiderlin-Wächter, German secretary of state since 1910, gambled that the Triple Entente had been weakened by Anglo-Russian rivalry in Persia. Accusing France of violating the Algeciras agreement, he reasoned, would free Germany of its treaty obligations. Acceptance of the new French advance would entitle his country to compensation. Although the French government had approached Germany at the end of June in order to reach an agreement, the German government, no master in the field of diplomatic strategy, decided that a show of force would provide better bargaining conditions. On July 1, 1911, the German chancellor, Theobald Bethmann-Hollweg, with the approval of the kaiser, sent the gunboat *Panther* to the western Moroccan port city of Agadir on the pretext of protecting German citizens.[48]

The "Sally of the Panther," as Europe soon termed the German action, created yet another war scare.[49] Most French socialists reacted resignedly rather than indignantly. Jaurès argued that Germany had merely followed the example of France in using the same superficial excuse—protection of its citizens—to gain the same imperialist ends: penetration and conquest.[50] "Algeciras has been thrown to the winds," Jaurès complained on July 3, "and there is no longer an atom of international good faith."[51]

In their desire to preserve the peace the socialists discovered an ally in the new head of government, Joseph Caillaux, who had come to power after the fall of the Monis government. Unlike Clemenceau, who believed in the inevitability of a Franco-German war, Caillaux accepted a policy of negotiation and appeasement (then a respectable word) with Germany. His work for peace was not based so much upon his pacifist nature as upon his faith in the practical efficacy of negotiations. He realized, too, that if France resorted to arms, Russia would hesitate to support its ally over a colonial dispute. On July 4, in response to an interpellation by Jaurès and Vaillant, Caillaux pledged to work for a peaceful settlement. Vaillant replied that peace was all the socialists wished and that they trusted the Caillaux government to maintain it.[52]

On July 11 the new foreign minister in Caillaux's government, Justin de Selves, appealed to the patience and patriotism of the socialists to allow the government to continue its negotiations with Germany without time-consuming parliamentary interruptions that might give Germany the impression of French disunity. Vaillant reiterated that peace was the foremost concern of his party, and Jaurès objected that the just and legal intervention of parliament was necessary to safeguard French interests. The socialists then demanded debate on the Agadir incident, but the Chamber rejected their demand by a vote of 476 to 77.[53]

During the critical months that followed, the negotiations were hamstrung by the intransigence of Kiderlin-Wächter, who demanded all of the French Congo as the price for French hegemony in Morocco. At one point Europe was brought disastrously close to war. England, fearing that Germany wanted a Moroccan port, warned that it would honor its commitments to

France. On July 21 the British chancellor of the exchequer, Lloyd George, delivered his famous "Mansion House Speech," approved by Prime Minister H. H. Asquith, in which the future war leader declared that Britain preferred war to a humiliating surrender over Morocco.

As the shadow of war fell across Europe, the French socialists, unable to continue their struggle against war in the Chamber of Deputies (then in summer recess), waged an unrelenting crusade for peace in the press, by public demonstrations, and through the International Socialist Bureau. On July 12, at a demonstration at the Manège Saint-Paul in Paris, the socialists condemned the capitalist governments of France, England, and Germany that threatened to involve the workers in war.[54] Throughout July and August, Allard, Sembat, and Thomas pleaded in the pages of *Humanité*[55] for a Franco-German rapprochement. On September 14 the Permanent Administrative Commission and representatives of the parliamentary group, including Vaillant, Sembat, and Thomas, met with the delegates of the International Socialist Bureau at Paris and decided that the Agadir crisis necessitated a full meeting. At the same time the socialists appealed to President Fallières to convoke parliament and joined with the leaders of the General Confederation of Labor in a manifesto condemning chauvinism in both France and Germany and appealing to the European proletariat to express its will for peace.[56]

While anxious for a peaceful settlement, the socialists rejected the prospect of a French protectorate in Morocco. "The socialists have consistently predicted this, and the government has just as consistently denied it," a bitter Sembat wrote on September 21. Now, during the recess of parliament, the government had capitulated to the Moroccan syndicate; henceforth, he said, the socialists had only scorn for governments that "speak their good faith with hand over heart" while pursuing a policy of colonial brigandage.[57] Three days later, at a socialist demonstration of 60,000 at the Aéro-Park in Paris, the socialist deputies Arthur Rozier (Seine), Voilin, Thomas, and Colly—along with Pierre Laval, who was to become socialist deputy for the Seine in 1914—denounced any plans for a Moroccan protectorate.[58] On September 25 the International Bureau, meeting at Zurich, could do no more than pass a resolution calling for international solidarity and the end of conflict over Morocco.[59]

By the end of October the second Moroccan crisis had passed, but the socialist agitation for peace had had little to do with the outcome. Caillaux had showed admirable skill in the negotiations, ignoring the anti-German sentiments in France that longed for a showdown. He had agreed to give Germany 250,000 square kilometers of the French Congo in return for a protectorate over Morocco, and on November 4 the Franco-German agreement of 1911 was signed.

The socialists greeted this treaty with mixed emotions. They were happy that the principle of international arbitration had triumphed over the principle of arms, but they deplored the protectorate. Jaurès and Sembat reflected these views in *Humanité*,[60] as did the socialist deputies Hubert Rouger (Gard), Edouard Barthe (Hérault), and Raffin Dugens in the Chamber on December 12. They argued that French colonial policy had cost the nation far more than it had gained; and Sixte Quenin excoriated the Radical party for repudiating its historic principles of anticolonialism and insisted that the socialists, by opposing the "criminal and ruinous" policy of the government, had merely "adopted an abandoned infant of Radicalism."[61]

The historic debate on the Franco-German agreement of 1911 was begun in the Chamber on December 14 and lasted through December 20. Throughout the often stormy debates the socialists, led by Jaurès, Vaillant, and Sembat, reiterated the arguments they had set forth for the past five years, especially in regard to governmental responsibility for the failure of peaceful penetration. Although they regretted that the treaty further involved France in a "dangerous and more ruinous colonial policy," the socialist speakers announced their intention to approve it because they considered it a "victory of negotiation over a barbaric resort to arms."[62] Vaillant stressed one of the main themes of the socialist speeches when he admitted that the Agadir crisis had found the socialists still insufficiently organized to prevent war. "This now becomes our supreme goal," Vaillant affirmed, "and when the next crisis appears the French socialists will do all that is necessary, all that is possible, for insuring that their peace efforts are effectual, and of this you may be certain, they will be effectual."[63]

On December 20 the Chamber ratified the Franco-German agreement by a vote of 393 to 36, despite 165 abstentions and the hostility of a number of deputies from the Right who believed that Caillaux had betrayed France by ceding part of the Congo. The vote revealed a split in socialist ranks. A majority of the party, led by Jaurès, Vaillant, and Sembat, voted to ratify the agreement. But twenty-four socialists abstained; and one deputy, Jean Bouhey-Allex, voted against. Compère-Morel justified the abstentions by explaining to the Chamber that he and his twenty-three friends intended "to let our bourgeois government take all the responsibility for a treaty that further engages France in a policy of ruinous colonial conquest."[64]

These abstentions were not the product of a serious split on foreign policy within the SFIO. Indeed, this was the first and last time from 1904 to 1914 that the parliamentary socialists were not in unanimous agreement on a major foreign policy issue. As Compère-Morel explained, the abstentions were only a protest for those socialists who, while happy that peace had been secured, could not vote for a protectorate or approve the gains of a policy of military expansion that the socialists had condemned for five years. The abstentions did reflect again, however, the traditional Guesdist hostility toward colonialism, for fourteen of the twenty-four deputies originally belonged to that faction.[65]

The socialists had applauded Caillaux's diplomatic skill during the crisis, but the clandestine manner in which negotiations had been carried out strengthened their hostility to secret diplomacy. When the Chamber convened on March 8, 1912, the new ministry of Raymond Poincaré was faced with three socialist interpellations, the first by the old Blanquist Ernest Roche and the other two by Jaurès and Vaillant. Roche proposed legislation "to prevent the concluding of treaties without the consent of parliament that are submitted for ratification when it is too late to modify them." Roche's argument that only the people could determine the best interests of France, typical of the socialist failure to understand the phenomenon of modern nationalism, was followed by a demand that the constitution be changed "to end the undemocratic regime of secret treaties." Jaurès supported these arguments, demanding the "revolutionizing" of French foreign policy and warning that the nation could no longer entrust its destinies to men who practice "the cult of antagonism" such as Delcassé, Pichon, and Clemenceau.[66] One week later Vaillant, Sembat, and Gabriel Ellen-Prévot, socialist deputy for Haute-Garonne, set forth similar arguments.[67]

A scandal concerning French colonial administration in Tunisia provided the socialists with another opportunity to denounce French colonial policy. In 1911 the League of the Rights of Man charged that the government had granted nearly two million acres of Tunisian land to certain privileged colons. On January 19, 1912, Charles Dumas, socialist deputy for Allier (and the author of *Libérez les indigènes ou renoncez aux colonies*, published in 1914), and Joseph Lagrosillière challenged the government on these concessions. Dumas charged that France had betrayed its role as protector and educator of the natives, and Lagrosillière delivered a long, documented account showing how corrupt administrators and financiers in Tunisia had abused their positions.[68] The following month Jaurès asked that a committee be formed to study the Tunisian question, but his request was rejected by a vote of 408 to 104.[69] The next day Lagrosillière requested that the government name a committee of thirty-three deputies to investigate firsthand the charges of colonial abuses in Tunisia and to recommend measures to ameliorate the political and economic condition of the natives, but his motion was likewise defeated by 402 votes to 99.[70] The socialists' comments on the Tunisian affair—the only example of their having discussed extensively the problems of French colonial possessions other than Morocco—complemented their ideas on Moroccan expansion. These ideas were best stated by Pressensé at the party congress at Brest in 1913, when he declared that while colonial abuse was inevitable, the natives should be treated in accordance with the humanitarian principles established in 1789.[71]

Socialist opposition to French colonial expansion in Morocco found its last expression in the vote on the Moroccan protectorate in July 1912, which was also the last time that colonial issues were discussed in the Chamber before the war. The socialists had already voiced their sentiment by voting against Poincaré's request for 50,000 francs to finance the trip of French ministers to Fez to negotiate the protectorate with the Moroccan sultan.[72] The treaty was signed on March 30 and presented for ratification on June 28. Vaillant, Sembat, Jaurès, Raffin Dugens, and Léon Betoulle (Haute-Vienne) led the socialists in denouncing the "immoral" protectorate treaty that was based upon brutal conquest.[73] On July 1 the Chamber ratified the treaty over unanimous socialist opposition.[74]

The campaign against the conquest of Morocco was the crisis point for pre-1914 French socialism. It accounts, to a large extent, for the continued growth of pacifism in the SFIO during the prewar years. To no other issue did the socialists devote so much time for so long. As their faith in peaceful penetration was shattered, their hope for Franco-German reconciliation undermined, their fear that capitalist exploitation of the

Moroccan natives would arouse religious and national passions against France justified by events, the French socialists fought a ceaseless and determined battle against the colonial policy of the government. In socialist caucuses, in public demonstrations, in the pages of *Humanité,* and at party congresses, they excoriated French policy in Morocco and predicted, often with amazing foresight, that it would lead to military conquest, thus weakening the chances of an already faltering peace. From the sword-rattling of Tangier to the coup of Agadir, the French socialists intervened thirty-one times in the Chamber of Deputies to urge the government to pursue a moderate and conciliatory foreign policy based upon reason; and just as many times their peace motions suffered frustrating defeats.

Despite this vigorous campaign, the French socialists never developed a positive, well-defined policy on colonialism. After the failure of the nebulous policy of peaceful penetration, they demanded recognition of Moroccan independence; but never once did they demand independence for any other French colony or denounce the colonial expansion of Germany or England. They incessantly attacked the abuses of the "colonial syndicate" in Morocco; but, with the exception of Tunisia, they never mentioned similar abuses in other French colonies, in Madagascar, Algeria, or Cochin-China. They never talked about reform of French administration in Annam, Tonkin, French Sudan, or the Congo Basin. Their action extended only to the passing of vague resolutions, such as the one approved by their national congress at Nancy, in August 1907, condemning colonial expansion as "an inherent crime in the capitalist regime searching for new markets." This lack of a well-formulated colonial policy robbed the French socialists of basic guiding principles during every Franco-German confrontation in Morocco. If they lacked such a policy, however, at all times they understood that negotiation in good faith was a rational alternative to a barbaric resort to arms over disputed areas; and they fervently and consistently de-

nounced the use of helpless, underdeveloped nations as chess-
boards upon which the Great Powers played their deadly game
of balance-of-power politics.

The second Moroccan crisis had revealed two further weaknesses in the socialist fight for peace. In light of socialist behavior in July 1914, which was a virtual repetition of their
action in the summer of 1911, they apparently failed to take
serious note of either of these weaknesses. The first was that if
war threatened, socialist political power in parliament could do
little to prevent it. Events transpired quickly, and the fate of
Europe was left in the hands of professional diplomats; parlia-
ments could only approve or disapprove accomplished facts.
The second was that the peace machinery of the French socialists and the Second International was impotent in the face of
war. The French socialists, like all European socialists, suffered
under the illusion that international goodwill, public demonstrations, and endless peace resolutions and manifestos could
compel the capitalist governments to come to terms. They could
and did talk about the general strike, but the talk ended with
ambiguous threats. One may argue, and rightly, that the idea of
a general strike to prevent war was a dubious, perhaps an impossible, idea to begin with. But a concrete plan for a strike in
factories and war industries, along with an expression of socialist determination to carry it out, might at least have provided
the French socialists with more effective bargaining power to
pressure the government to implement a moderate foreign policy. Abel Ferry's *Carnet B*, which contained the names of insur-
rectionaries to be arrested in case of war,[75] indicates that the
government would not have considered such a threat to be an
empty one.

The answer to why the socialists failed to draw up a concrete plan for a general strike indicates what the socialist response would have been if war had broken out in the summer of
1911. A first glance at socialist propaganda during the second

75

Moroccan crisis suggests that the socialists were determined to prevent the government from plunging the nation into war over Morocco. They pleaded for peace, and they denounced the French actions that had provoked the crisis; but the socialists were patriots at the same time, and never once did they threaten to subvert the war effort if conflict broke out. In his memoirs Joseph Paul-Boncour relates that shortly after the Agadir crisis General Messimy said to Jaurès: "Well, Jaurès, we avoided war. We did all we could to avoid it. But if, despite our action, Germany had forced us into it, what would you have done?" Jaurès supposedly answered: "Just what Gambetta did. I would have toured the country to activate the national defense."[76] This may only have been one of Jaurès's off-the-cuff remarks, but it reflected the patriotic sentiments of most French socialists in 1911; and it is likely that if war had broken out then, it would have been pictured, as in 1914, as a defensive war. In the latter case an affirmative response from the socialists had long been determined by their own patriotic attitudes.

V

NATIONAL SELF-DETERMINATION

AND OPPRESSED PEOPLES:

ALSACE-LORRAINE, TURKEY, AND

THE BALKANS

The attitudes of the French socialists toward national self-determination reflected a dualism produced by two conflicting aims. The socialists expressed hope that oppressed peoples would someday be victorious in their struggle for freedom, but they emphasized that this victory must not endanger the peace.

This dualism on the part of the socialists is illustrated by their attitude toward the recovery of Alsace-Lorraine. Shortly after 1871 the French socialists voiced hopes for the recovery of these "lost colonies."[1] As the passions stirred by the Franco-Prussian War died down in the fifteen years following 1871, the socialists, like most Frenchmen, talked less and less of the eventual recovery of these territories; and the Boulangist episode of 1889 seemed to dissolve any remaining thoughts within socialist ranks of recovering Alsace-Lorraine.[2] Jaurès wrote in the *Petite République* of December 5, 1901, that France "should abandon without one afterthought the idea of revanche."[3] On November 23, 1902, in the same newspaper, he condemned chauvinistic politicians, declaring that "all politics of revanche are nothing more than a figure of rhetoric."[4] On January 23, 1903, he told the Chamber that Alsace-Lorraine would regain its freedom when democratic government had expanded throughout Europe, an opinion held also by Guesde and the majority of the socialists.[5]

During the period from 1904 to 1906, Alsace-Lorraine was seldom mentioned in the Chamber of Deputies and did not appear to be a germinal issue in French political life or foreign policy. Indeed, only one socialist speaker ever mentioned Alsace-Lorraine between 1904 and 1906; and that was again Jaurès, who told the Chamber on November 10, 1904, that while the French socialists would not abandon the right violated thirty-four years ago, they had no intention of appealing to force to redress the wrong of a crime of force. Applauded by the socialists, Jaurès stated that if France, for the sake of Alsace-Lorraine, should refuse a rapprochement with Germany, prospects for a European peace would be jeopardized.[6] An official German protest to Jaurès's phrase "a crime of force"[7] revealed the inconsistency of socialist attempts to preserve a spirit of internationalism in their foreign policy attitudes while placing national honor and security above all else.

Between 1907 and the outbreak of war the French socialists continued to denounce the idea of a war of revenge against Germany over Alsace-Lorraine, just as they had done in conjunction with their attack on French policy in Morocco. On November 26, 1908, Pressensé spoke of "the crime committed against human rights in 1870, which no one resents more than the French socialist party"; and he mourned the loss of the "historic role of Alsace, whereby Alsace had served as an intermediary between French and German culture." But he quickly added that socialism condemned the idea of revenge by arms, and he attacked the public school textbooks that "fill the minds of French youth with the poison of revenge."[8]

Jaurès, especially, waged a continuing battle in the Chamber and in the press against the war of revenge advocated by chauvinistic politicians and journalists who refused to forget the dark memories of 1870. In January 1909 he warned the Chamber of the futility of such a policy, contending that the triumph of social democracy, not only in Alsace-Lorraine but also among the suppressed peoples of Poland, Finland, Ireland, Cuba, Bosnia and Herzegovina, and Morocco, would be "the great revenge of France and democracy."[9] At the same time, he also denounced chauvinism in Germany. He praised the courage of the people of Alsace-Lorraine in the face of the brutality of Prussian administration, and he pleaded that Germany likewise forget the past and allow Alsace-Lorraine to continue in its French tradition.[10] When Germany granted Alsace-Lorraine a state constitution in 1911, Jaurès praised it as "an evident step in progress toward democracy," but regretted that it did not provide full autonomy.[11] The day following the notorious Saverne incident in November 1913, when a German officer arrested a group of civilians who had clashed with a number of young officers, Jaurès wrote, in the *Dépêche de Toulouse* of November 28, 1913, that the incident revealed the sentiments of those in Alsace whose "hearts are still with France and its traditions." "These are sentiments," Jaurès remarked bitterly, "that the stupid, arrogant, and odious Pan-Germanists are incapable of understanding."[12]

Other party leaders, such as Allard and Vaillant, argued along similar lines. In the former's view the concept of revanche implied nothing less than a war against Europe to redress the

settlement of 1815;[13] and in his plea for Franco-German reconciliation at the party congress at Brest in March 1913, Vaillant,
like Pressensé, spoke of the historic role of Alsace-Lorraine as
a bond between French and German culture. Gustave Hervé contended that the problem of Alsace-Lorraine was the only obstacle to a Franco-German rapprochement; this difficulty would
be resolved if Germany granted autonomy to Alsace-Lorraine.
Hervé proposed, therefore, that the parliamentary group demand from the government of Raymond Poincaré an accord
with Germany based on that compromise.[14] Hervé's constructive
idea (one of the few of his political career), though applauded
by the delegates, was never put to the test.

Thus, while the French socialists regretted the loss of
Alsace-Lorraine, a loss which they regarded as a weakening of
a historic link between French and German culture, they consistently denounced the idea of a war of revenge as the means to
liberate this disputed area. They warned that chauvinism in
either France or Germany only prolonged old hatreds, undermined the possibility of Franco-German reconciliation, endan-
gered the peace, and destroyed hopes for a cordial solution to
the problem of Alsace-Lorraine. The socialists looked to a slow
and peaceful victory of social democracy in Alsace-Lorraine,
preceded by the hoped-for autonomy. This, they advocated,
would both preserve the peace and usher in a new era of justice.

The dualism in the French socialists' views on national self-
determination is also illustrated by their attitudes toward the
problems of the Balkans, Turkey, and eastern Europe. The
socialists often expressed sympathy for the peoples of these
areas, suffering under the heel of insensitive rulers, plagued
with internal chaos, and torn by the rivalry of the Great Powers.
In April 1908, for example, Pressensé condemned Austro-
Russian expansion in the Balkans and warned that Balkan disorders, such as the conflict between Greeks and Bulgarians in
Macedonia, only whetted the imperialist appetites of the Great

Powers. He urged the French government to support the English proposals of December 1907 for military and financial reform in Macedonia, which Austria and Russia had rejected.[15] The following June, in an editorial in *Humanité*, Jaurès deplored the human misery caused by the Balkan disorders and castigated the government for its failure to support the English reform proposals.[16]

Revolution in the Ottoman Empire the next month aggravated the situation in the troubled Balkan peninsula even further. On July 25, 1908, the notorious Sultan Abdul Hamid was swept from power. The "Young Turks," many of whom were energetic young military leaders trained by German army officers, rode to power on the crest of a wave of Turkish nationalism and instituted reforms to cure the Sick Man of Europe.

Turkish possessions in the Balkans soon felt the impact of the Young Turk Revolution; and Russia and Austria, as Pressensé had feared, resolved to exploit the situation. On September 15 Russian Foreign Minister Isvolsky and Austrian Foreign Minister Alois von Aehrenthal met at Buchlau and verbally agreed that Russia would recognize Austrian annexation of Bosnia and Herzegovina if Austria would not oppose the opening of the Straits to Russia. Aehrenthal's action was motivated by the Dual Monarchy's fear of Serbian ambitions in Bosnia and Herzegovina, which nominally formed a part of the Turkish Empire, although Austria had ruled these areas as a virtual protectorate since 1878.

Austria found the opportunity to carry out the plan on October 5, when Bulgaria declared its independence. Aehrenthal acted quickly and annexed Bosnia and Herzegovina the next day. When Russia attempted to gain control of the Straits, Vienna refused its support. Russian indignation at this betrayal almost certainly would have led to war had not Russia still been suffering from the aftereffects of its disastrous war with Japan. Thus, by the middle of October 1908, the elements of July 1914

81

were beginning to form. A frustrated Russia clutched for its share of the decaying Sick Man, and an incensed Serbia spoiled for a showdown with Austria.[17]

The French socialists responded to these events with a severe condemnation of Austrian and Russian imperialism. Jaurès termed the Austrian move "the clumsy action of a flock of birds of prey, circling over the Turkish people."[18] He proposed an international congress of the Powers to deal with the Balkan problem,[19] but he feared that France's leadership in such a congress had been undermined by French aggression in Morocco.[20] On October 12, 1908, the International Socialist Bureau met at Brussels, with France represented by Vaillant and Alexander Bracke, a member of the National Council of the SFIO. Vaillant proposed a motion, which was adopted unanimously, condemning Russia and Austria for stirring up religious and national passions in the Balkans.[21] The next day Victor Adler, the Austrian socialist leader, added an amendment specifically condemning the annexation of Bosnia and Herzegovina.[22] A few days later, at their national party congress at Toulouse, the French socialists approved another motion denouncing the sovereigns of Austria, Russia, and Bulgaria for their Balkan aggressions.[23] Neither the International nor the French socialists proposed any redress for past actions or preventives for future wrongs. Once again the socialist peace effort had been limited to innocuous motions and resolutions.

After the Bosnian crisis, French socialist foreign policy attitudes reflected a marked hostility to the Dual Monarchy. In January 1909 Jaurès warned the Chamber that Austrian designs in the Balkans could lead to war, and he advocated the establishment of democratic regimes in this troubled area.[24] In the press he complained that the Bosnian crisis had been caused by "the lawless coup of Baron von Aehrenthal and the hypocritical pretensions of Russian diplomacy,"[25] and he demanded that Austria provide Bosnia and Herzegovina with constitutional governments.[26] Allemane and Bracke likewise feared Austrian aggression and prophetically warned that a localized clash between Austria and Serbia would erupt into a general European war.[27] At the sixth party congress of the SFIO (Saint-Etienne, April 11-14, 1909) the French socialists again condemned the Austrian annexation, criticized Russian imperialism, and praised the peace efforts of the Austrian and Serbian socialists.[28]

The socialists proposed a Slavic federation as the only sensible solution to the Balkan problem. Speaking for his party in December 1909, Pressensé told the Chamber that a Balkan federation would repel Austrian and Russian aggression and enable the Slavic peoples to realize their national ambitions. The Serbs, he said, were a passionate, often a belligerent, people; but they were also heroic and had suffered greatly under the heel of Austria. Pressensé concluded by criticizing Aehrenthal's foreign policy as a menace to the peace and by proposing that the Powers meet soon to arrange for the creation of a Balkan federation.[29] Bracke supported this idea, suggesting that Serbia, Bosnia, Herzegovina, Montenegro, and Dalmatia combine to form an independent state, either as a federation or as an autonomous part of the Austro-Hungarian Empire.[30] At the Second International congress at Copenhagen in September 1910, Vaillant led the French delegation in proposing a motion which faithfully reflected these principles and aspirations of the French socialists.[31]

The socialists realized that the Balkan problem was inextricably linked to the difficulties of the faltering Ottoman Empire. They were deeply sympathetic with the Young Turk Revolution and believed that it was the first step toward the abolition of Turkish despotism and the realization of social justice for the suffering Turkish people. Pressensé affirmed in the Chamber on November 26, 1908, that his party fully supported the Young Turk Revolution, and he entreated the French government to protect Turkey from Austrian and Russian

83

encroachments so the Young Turks could complete a program of reform.[32] Jaurès likewise pictured the Young Turk Revolution as a great national and liberal movement.[33] He argued that "it involved a part of the moral patrimony of France itself," and once again he reflected the patriotism underlying his foreign policy outlook when he added that the revolution benefited France since the deposed Abdul Hamid had given Germany a favored position in his empire.[34]

Socialist hopes for a new Turkish national state that could lead an awakened Moslem world were sorely disappointed during the next few years. In September of 1911 Italy, anxious to enter the colonial race by acquiring Tripoli, declared war on Turkey, which was determined to retain its last possession in North Africa. The Italian aggression angered the French socialists. Sembat wrote that "Italy has followed the law of force,"[35] and Jaurès termed the attack "a work of brigandage."[36] Louis Debreuilh, the secretary of the Permanent Administrative Commission of the SFIO, demanded that the Powers restrain the "Italian pirates."[37]

The French parliamentary socialists and the various federations of the SFIO worked closely with the International Socialist Bureau to arouse European opinion against the Italian attack (which had occurred at the height of the second Moroccan crisis). On September 14, 1911, Camille Huysmans, secretary of the International Bureau, and members of the parliamentary group and the Permanent Administrative Commission voted a resolution urging the immediate convocation of the Bureau.[38] The next day the parliamentary socialists issued a manifesto calling for the convocation of parliament,[39] and from September 21 to 24 numerous federations of the SFIO staged peace rallies at which socialist speakers denounced the Italian attack.[40] On September 23, during an International Bureau meeting at Zurich, the socialist representatives of fourteen nations condemned the Italian attack on Turkey.[41] Eleven days later the Permanent

Administrative Commission issued another manifesto condemning the Italian massacre of women and children in Tripoli.[42] These measures had little effect, and by October of 1912 Italy had occupied Tripoli and the Dodecanese Islands. Jaurès viewed the Turkish defeat as "the unfortunate elimination of Turkey from Europe, the loss of the supreme chance of the Moslems to adapt themselves to Europe."[43]

Sympathy for the Moslem world was one of Jaurès's central foreign policy ideas, and the socialists' speeches on Morocco indicated that the majority of them shared this sympathy. In his speeches and editorials Jaurès foresaw what few statesmen of his time understood: the Moslem world, having breathed the air of nationalism, was suffering the birth pangs of the modern age. Since the days of Francis I, France had had important political and economic ties with Turkey and its possessions in Asia Minor and the Balkans; and as early as March 1890 Jaurès had urged that France maintain its tradition of protection of these areas.[44] He often contended that France must either renounce its imperialism or repudiate its "moral role" in the Moslem world;[45] if France would protect Turkish liberties and the integrity of the Moslem world, it would gain world respect.[46] In November 1908 Jaurès condemned Russian expansion into Persia and lamented that France's Moroccan policy had abolished the moral basis for restraining this expansion.[47] In the Chamber on January 13, 1911, he denounced the despotism of the corrupt Persian shahs and their ignoble ministers, but praised the ancient Persian culture; and he condemned Russia and Germany for their penetration in Persia, along with "liberal England" for associating itself with this policy.[48] Jaurès's hopes for French action to aid the Moslem world were an expression of both his patriotism and his deep humanitarianism.

The Italo-Turkish War aggravated the tensions in eastern Europe. The helplessness of a defeated Turkey sharpened the territorial appetites of the Balkan states; and in October 1912

Serbia, Bulgaria, Greece, and Montenegro declared war on Turkey. On November 8 King Constantine led a victorious Greek army into Salonika. Three weeks later a Serbian army, marching southwest through Albania, occupied the seaport of Durazzo on the Adriatic.[49]

The socialists now witnessed the creation of a Balkan federation, but it was obviously not the kind they had hoped for. Jaurès viewed it as a belligerent confederation, "the response to the hypocritical formulas used by the Powers."[50] In the Chamber of Deputies in January of the preceding year, he had discussed the Balkan problem at length, warning that such events might occur. Austrian and Russian imperialism had aroused Balkan national passions, "using the Turkish Revolution to intervene and create grave new problems for the national liberty and independence of Turkey." Aehrenthal had resorted to "cheap polemics to justify the brutal annexation of Bosnia and Herzegovina"; and if war came in the Balkans, it would come "not because the nations are anxious to declare war but because underhanded diplomacy, lies, and intrigues have created panic and misunderstanding."[51]

With the outbreak of the First Balkan War, one of Jaurès's worst fears had materialized. He pleaded with Russia and Austria to renounce secrecy and intrigue and to proclaim their intention to respect the independence of Turkey.[52] He argued that if the Balkan war engulfed Europe, Russia and Austria would be equally responsible;[53] and he demanded that the International Socialist Bureau convene, contending that if the Powers could not prevent a Balkan war, they certainly could not expect to localize it.[54]

French socialist agitation for peace during the next three months was a virtual repetition of their efforts during the second Moroccan crisis. Sembat, Jaurès, and Compère-Morel waged a daily campaign in *Humanité* against the war, demanding united French, British, and German action to stop the fighting.[55] On

October 17, 1912, the parliamentary group issued a manifesto placing the blame for the war on capitalist intrigue and bourgeois diplomacy and proclaiming the international socialist movement the only effectual peace force in Europe.[56] Eleven days later the International Socialist Bureau met at Brussels, with France represented by Jaurès, Vaillant, Jean Longuet, and Pierre Renaudel. The delegates agreed to Jaurès's proposal for an emergency congress of the Second International, which was accordingly scheduled for the following month.[57] When the International congress met at the Swiss city of Basel on November 25, Jaurès and Vaillant pleaded for peace in the Balkans, as they had done at a socialist rally of 100,000 in Paris one week earlier.[58] Jaurès and the French delegation proposed an autonomous Albania with a Balkan democratic federation;[59] and although the delegates agreed with this proposal, they could do little more than issue an antiwar manifesto, as drawn up by Jaurès, expressing confidence in the ability of the Second International to prevent war.[60]

The socialist agitation in France had little influence on the actions of Raymond Poincaré's government. Poincaré told the Chamber on December 21 that the solution to the Balkan problem lay in negotiation, not in the agitation of international groups. His government, he said, had used its influence for peace by urging Vienna "to heed the principle of territorial disinterestedness in the Balkans." The premier then praised the Conference of Ambassadors at London that was seeking to end the Balkan war, and he promised that France would continue to use its diplomatic and moral influence to maintain the peace.

Vaillant responded for the socialists, thanking Poincaré for his assurances and promising full socialist support if he continued to act for peace. But Vaillant warned, to the applause of the Extreme Left, that his party would call a general strike if the government involved France in an aggressive war. Jaurès also praised Poincaré's efforts and those of the Conference of

Ambassadors at London, and he urged that France take the lead in seeking out and eliminating the causes of Balkan disputes.[61]

By May 1913 peace had temporarily quieted the Balkans. The Conference of Ambassadors drew up a treaty which stripped Turkey of virtually all of its European possessions and provided for the creation of an independent Albania. In the Chamber of Deputies, Vaillant reflected the generally favorable socialist reaction to the treaty when he expressed hope that the Balkans would never trouble the peace of Europe again. But he emphasized that before a permanent Balkan peace could be established, the real cause of Balkan unrest—Austrian and Russian imperialism—must be eliminated; and he criticized the government for its continued capitulation to the latter.[62]

Within a few weeks the Balkan volcano erupted again when Bulgaria, dissatisfied with the peace settlement, turned on its former allies. This Second Balkan War ended in September 1913, with the defeat of Bulgaria. During the summer of 1913 Pressensé wrote two lengthy articles in *Humanité* condemning Bulgaria and urging the collective intervention of Europe to stop the war.[63] Other than this, the French socialists paid little attention to this second phase of the war, for their attention and energies from March to July were concentrated upon what they considered to be one of the most important tasks of their careers —the campaign against the three-year law.

French socialist attitudes toward the problems of Alsace-Lorraine, Turkey, and the Balkan states reflected three important foreign policy principles: sympathy with the quest for national identity and security by the oppressed peoples and emerging underdeveloped nations, hostility toward the ruthless imperialism of the Powers that exploited the weaknesses of these nations, and a strong conviction that France should exercise a preponderant moral role in bringing peace and justice to these areas. In accord with their campaign for a Franco-German rapprochement, the French socialists advocated autonomy for

Alsace-Lorraine as the best means to resolve the uncertainty of the status of that area and to eliminate a major point of international tension. Regarding the Moslem world, they hoped that with the aid of France a reformed and vigorous new Turkey could lead all awakening Moslem nations into the modern age, protected from internal abuse and guarded against the encroachment of the Powers. And the socialists understood, perhaps better than anyone else, that the Slavic struggle in the Balkans for national identity had collided with Russian and Austrian ambitions. They knew that stability in Europe would never be assured as long as those ambitions went unchecked and as long as the Slavic national ideal went unfulfilled. Despite their repeated parliamentary failures, their proposals for a Balkan federation, consented to by all the Powers and created within the framework of a peaceful Europe, pointed to a sane and realistic solution.

THE LAST FIGHT FÓR PEACE:

SUMMER 1914

The socialist fight for peace paid off in the elections of April and May 1914. Pledged to a continued struggle against militarism and war and allied with the Radical-Socialists, the SFIO emerged as the second largest party in the Chamber of Deputies. Most students of the period are agreed that the election battle was waged over the repeal of the three-year law and that the unprecedented 1,398,000 votes for the socialist peace platform demonstrated that Poincaré's brand of nationalism found no place in the hearts of a significant number of Frenchmen.[1] The 101 new socialist deputies thus entered the Chamber with high optimism. They hoped that with the help of Caillaux and the Radical-Socialists the three-year law would be repealed, and they believed that the growing power of the SFIO and the SPD would soon compel the governments of France and Germany to come to terms. Also, they counted on improving the peace machinery of the Second International in order to restrain any capitalist government that threatened to strike its neighbor.

But time was short. On June 28, 1914, Archduke Francis Ferdinand, heir to the throne of Austria-Hungary, was felled by an assassin's bullet in the streets of Sarajevo. Balkan passions had fomented yet another crisis; but the accounts of the murder in *Humanité* gave no warnings of imminent war, as they had done during the second Moroccan crisis or the First Balkan War.[2] After all, two Moroccan crises and two Balkan Wars had passed without a major conflict; and the French socialists, like most Europeans, believed that reasonable men would talk their way out of this crisis just as they had done for the past forty-four years. Thus, Marcel Sembat concluded that the murder was just "one more act in the brutal Balkan drama" whose first act the Vienna diplomats had written when Austria had annexed Bosnia and Herzegovina.[3]

Ten days after the assassination the government made its request for 400,000 francs to defray the cost of the proposed state visit of President Poincaré and Premier Viviani to St. Petersburg. The socialists were suspicious of the purpose of the trip, fearing that Poincaré intended to arrange new loans or to strengthen the secret clauses of the Franco-Russian Alliance, thus involving the nation in the Balkan imbroglio. Jaurès protested that the trip would strengthen Czarist oppression of the Russian people, and he argued that if the Duma had succeeded, the alliance with Russia might have been transformed into an instrument of peace. Poincaré insisted that the visit was in the interests of peace; and despite unanimous socialist opposition, the Chamber approved credits for the voyage by a vote of 428 to 106.[4]

While Austria, with the support of Germany, plotted its revenge against Serbia, the French socialists assembled at Paris in July for their twelfth national congress. Among the observers were the German Marxist theoretician Karl Liebknecht and the Reichstag deputy Georg Weill, both of whom condemned chauvinism in France and Germany and voiced their hopes that Alsace-Lorraine would not forever divide the two countries.[5] On July 15 the delegates began three days of intensive debate over the course of action to be followed if war broke out. This debate was not provoked by the expectation of an immediate conflict over the assassination at Sarajevo, but in order to determine the French socialist position when the matter came up for debate at the next month's International congress at Vienna. Guesde, aging and barely recuperated from a lengthy illness, again opposed the idea of any kind of strike, arguing that it would be "a crime of high treason against socialism." Hervé supported Guesde and perceptively pointed out that the patriotism of the workers would prevent their ever accepting the idea of a strike. But Jaurès and Vaillant skillfully defended the strike, arguing that it was the best means to impose arbitration upon an aggressor nation, which the socialists defined simply as the nation refusing to accept arbitration. Their intervention overruled Guesde's objections, and the party congress reaffirmed the peace resolutions of Stuttgart, Copenhagen, and Basel, and formally declared the socialist intention to call a general strike if the government of France waged an aggressive war.[6] This motion was the most strongly worded such statement to date. Whether the workers would support it in a crisis remained to be seen.

Europe became aware of the seriousness of the situation only on July 24, when the world learned of the Austrian ultimatum to Serbia. Jaurès termed it "an act without precedent in the annals of diplomacy . . . intended first to humiliate and then to abolish Serbia."[7] On July 25 Serbia responded to the ultimatum, agreeing to most of the demands. Vienna considered the reply unsatisfactory and recalled its ambassador. Within two days Serbia had begun mobilization and awaited the inevitable Austrian onslaught.

The French socialists were now painfully aware of the danger confronting Europe, but they hoped that the impending conflict could be localized. At Lyon on July 26 Jaurès, speaking in behalf of the candidacy of the socialist Marius Moutet, pleaded for arbitration and attributed the precipitation of the crisis to the aggressive policies of France, Austria, Russia, and Germany.[8] The next day the parliamentary socialists issued a manifesto condemning Austrian belligerence and cautioning that Russian intervention "would stimulate Pan-German aggression." Warning that the French socialists would not support a war produced by the function of secret treaties, the manifesto exhorted the Powers to restrain their allies and recommended the mediation proposed by England.[9] At the same time the German socialist leaders issued a similar manifesto, protesting "the frivolous provocation to war of the Austro-Hungarian government."[10]

On July 28 Austria declared war on Serbia. That same day the French parliamentary socialists issued a more strongly worded manifesto, suggesting that Russian intervention would only inflame existing passions and again exhorting the government to follow the English proposals for mediation.[11] Although the French government was supporting these proposals, the socialists felt that it was backing them too halfheartedly and that it would in the final analysis capitulate again to Russian ambitions. The Permanent Administrative Commission demanded, therefore, that the French government restrain its Russian ally and declared that "France must not be thrown into the Serbian conflict by the arbitrary interpretation of the secret clauses of treaties."[12]

On July 29 and 30 the International Socialist Bureau met at Brussels to plan its peace strategy, with Jaurès, Sembat, Guesde, Vaillant, Longuet, and Renaudel representing the

SFIO. The Bureau decided that the next congress of the International, scheduled for Vienna in August, should meet instead at Paris on August 9. This congress, like the peace hopes of the delegates, never materialized. Despite the abundant goodwill and the outward show of solidarity, the impotence of the Second International in the face of war was only too clear. Victor Adler complained to the Bureau that the war against Serbia had such popular support that the Austrian socialists could do little to stop it. Hugo Haase, chairman of the SPD, affirmed, on the other hand, that he and his colleagues would oppose German intervention in the Serbian dispute, even should Russia enter. In the next few days, however, it became apparent that Haase had not spoken for the majority of his party. Jaurès assured the delegates that the French government was working to preserve the peace; and he warned that if the governments of Europe violated the peace, a war-weary proletariat would rise against and destroy its former masters.[13] The next day the Bureau signed still another antiwar manifesto;[14] and shortly before leaving Brussels, Jaurès, refusing to believe that the moment of truth had finally come, told the Belgian socialist leader Emile Vandervelde: "It will be like Agadir: there will be ups and downs, but things cannot but be settled."[15]

While in Brussels, Jaurès had telegraphed an editorial to *Humanité* calling for a demonstration on August 2 to proclaim socialist determination to preserve the peace during the present crisis and to demand of the government that the danger of war be resolved by arbitration.[16] After returning to Paris on the evening of July 30, a tired Jaurès led a socialist delegation to Premier Viviani to plead that he restrain Russia and continue his efforts for peace. The delegation expressed satisfaction with the government's decision to withdraw French troops ten kilometers from the frontier and with its promise that those whose names appeared on the *Carnet B* would not be arrested.[17] Viviani said nothing of the French pledge of July 28 to support

Russia, however; and he also failed to mention that he had ordered the police to break up any antiwar demonstrations.[18]

The next day the socialists redoubled their peace efforts. In the press Jaurès pleaded for *sang-froid nécessaire.*[19] That afternoon France learned that Germany, in response to the Russian mobilization, had proclaimed its *drohende Kriegsgefahr,* the "imminent danger of war." That evening another socialist delegation, composed of Jaurès, Longuet, Renaudel, Bracke, Marcel Cachin, and Albert Bedouce, attempted to repeat to Viviani its pleas for arbitration. The premier could not see the persistent deputies, for at 7:00 P.M. the German ambassador, Baron Wilhelm von Schoen, had informed him of the German ultimatum to Russia demanding suspension of mobilization or war. Schoen had also demanded that France indicate within eighteen hours whether or not it would remain neutral in case of a Russo-German war. Unable to reach the premier, the apprehensive socialist group turned to Louis Malvy, minister of the interior, and Abel Ferry, the under-secretary of state. The delegation asked once more if the government was pressuring Russia to stay out of the Balkans, but it received only evasive answers to the effect that the ministers were doing everything possible to preserve the faltering peace. Jaurès warned Ferry that "we will clear our party of any guilt; we will struggle against war to the very end." The under-secretary replied prophetically, "No, you won't be able to continue. You will be assassinated on the nearest streetcorner."[20] It was on this occasion that Jaurès, frustrated by the banal efforts that were passing for statesmenship in this critical hour, retorted to Ferry, "You are all the victims of Isvolsky and Russian intrigue; we are going to denounce all of you light-headed ministers, even should we be shot."[21]

Less than three hours had passed before Ferry's prophecy came true. Later in the evening Jaurès and some of his friends on the staff of *Humanité* were dining at the Café Croissant before composing the next day's issue. A young nationalist, Raoul

Villain, consumed with hatred for the socialist tribune's pacifist efforts, assassinated Jaurès as he dined. The most powerful voice for peace in France was now stilled. But the socialists continued their efforts for a settlement, despite the German ultimatum to France and Russia and despite the seeming resignation of the Powers to the inevitability of war. The next day the saddened deputies met at the Palais Bourbon and attempted to coordinate their peace efforts with the SPD through its representative, Hermann Müller. Müller suggested that both parties vote against war credits, but he warned that such action must be bilateral and that each party must decide for itself. It was a fruitless conference. Within a few hours French mobilization was decreed, and Müller departed for Berlin.[22]

To this point the French socialists had fought a strong battle for peace. They had demanded that the government restrain Russia and renew attempts for mediation. Their propaganda indicated that they would oppose France's being drawn into a war on the basis of the secret clauses of the Franco-Russian Alliance. They had waged a ceaseless battle for peace in the press, in public speeches, and through the Second International. Jaurès had told the International Bureau that his government was working for peace, and the French socialists had given no indication that they would halt their campaign. On July 31, at the meeting with Ferry, Jaurès had reaffirmed his party's determination to struggle against the war to the very end.

But socialist reservations began to melt away on August 2, and the event that may have prompted this change of attitude was the German invasion of Luxemburg on the same day. Like all of France, the socialists realized that this was the first step to invasion of *la patrie*. Here was the unprovoked attack, the great war of defense, the call for all citizens to take up arms to drive out the invader. The socialists had long agreed that in such a war they would not betray the France they considered the mother of revolution, the land where in 1789, as Jaurès had

96

written in his *Histoire socialiste de la révolution française,* the
tide of liberty had swept away the decadent Old Regime and
prepared the way for the advent of the proletariat.[23]

On August 2 the socialist leaders met at the Salle Wagram.
Vaillant, Sembat, Longuet, Cachin, and Compère-Morel again
denounced Austrian, Russian, and German aggression; and
Vaillant declared that "the French socialists, in the presence of
an aggressor, will do their duty for *la patrie,* for the Republic,
and for the International."[24] But even then the socialists had not
completely resigned themselves to war, for this group again
affirmed socialist determination "to safeguard unto the end the
hope for a peaceful settlement and to maintain our reservations
upon the obligations of secret treaties."[25] Even the next day,
after Germany, with the support of the SPD, had declared war
on France, Vaillant led another socialist delegation to Viviani
to plead for new mediation proposals, only to be informed that
the German ambassador had already left.[26]

On the morning of August 4 the socialists paid their last
tribute to their greatest peacemaker. After the funeral they jour-
neyed to the Chamber of Deputies, where Paul Deschanel, the
foreign policy spokesman for the Right, delivered an eloquent
tribute to the fallen socialist leader who had been his chief an-
tagonist on virtually every domestic and foreign policy issue for
the last twenty years. Then, despite their repeated warnings over
the past ten years that the secret clauses of the Franco-Russian
Alliance would someday bring France to this dreaded moment,
the socialists joined with their fellow deputies in a unanimous
Chamber approval of war credits.[27]

Thus, within a matter of days the socialist dream of a
world where wise men no longer resorted to bloody wars was
dissolved. The French socialists learned too late that their peace
resolutions and antiwar propaganda could not stave off this hour
of tragedy. The Second International had turned out to be a
mere facade when, on August 3, the German socialists had voted

for war credits.[28] As the nations of Europe lunged at each other, only the socialists of two countries—Serbia and Russia—remained faithful to the utopia of peace. After a prolonged and vigorous campaign to maintain the peace, and only after German troops had taken the first aggressive step, the French socialists decided to support France against the aggressor.

VII

CONCLUSION

The collapse of the Second International on the eve of the
First World War pointedly demonstrated the superficiality of
European socialist unity. The outbreak of war showed that blind
faith in international goodwill coupled with a stubborn refusal
to face reality were no adequate foundations upon which to con-
struct an effectual program of peace. The French socialists
shared in this uncritical optimism, but to disparage their stead-
fast pursuit of peace by pointing to their failure in 1914 is to
ignore many constructive and realistic ideas they had preached
for ten years. Between 1904 and 1914 the struggle against war
was the major task for the French socialists. Peace was their

dominant theme, clearly and without ambiguity, in almost every foreign policy speech. The French socialists suffered many illusions as to the best means to prevent war, but their proposals in the Chamber of Deputies reflected a profound understanding of the threats that confronted Europe. They recognized the inevitability of conflict as long as nations continued to arm; and they understood that the only road to a durable peace lay in a moderate and conciliatory foreign policy, based upon international reconciliation and a willingness to arbitrate differences. Their denunciations of armaments and military expenditures, their attempts to resolve each international crisis by arbitration, their consistent opposition to every government action that might endanger the peace, their active sympathy for oppressed peoples, and their repeated pleas for Franco-German reconciliation sharply distinguished the SFIO from any other political or parliamentary group.

The French socialists usually met in caucus before the Chamber sessions opened and selected the speaker or speakers who would represent the party on any important issue. The party had a kind of foreign policy cabinet, composed mainly of Jaurès, Vaillant, Sembat, Allard, Pressensé, Thomas, Rouanet, and Willm; but it was Jaurès who was selected as the group's spokesman more often than any of the others. Daniel Halévy once asked, "What is the [French socialist] party?" Answering his own question, he declared, "I will define it in one word: It was Jaurès. It was his reflection. He created it. He kept it together."[1] Halévy overstated the case, but his point was well taken. Between 1904 and 1914 Jaurès made more speeches and received more international attention than all the other parliamentary socialists combined. Jaurès was the source of ideas for the French socialists; and his speeches to the Chamber, his retorts and deviations, his excursions into history and philosophy, and his perceptive understanding of men and events revealed a mind that grasped the critical issues of the period—a mind

100

creative, imaginative, and original enough to influence the foreign policy ideas of other socialists.

In their speeches and voting habits during this period the French socialists were generally of one accord—with only minor aberrations—in their approach to foreign policy issues. At the party congresses at Limoges and Nancy, Hervéism and Guesdism threatened to divide the party's approach to peace, but met with little success. Within the Chamber of Deputies the socialists minimized their differences, and there were few occasions on which the pre-1905 disunity manifested itself in foreign policy matters. Despite this parliamentary unity, socialist foreign policy attitudes failed to exert any decisive influence upon the course of French foreign policy. Such influence had ended when the socialists withdrew from Combes's *Bloc des Gauches* (in which Jaurès had been the most prominent member) in the fall of 1904. From 1904 to 1914 the Radical and Radical-Socialist majority usually overruled socialist objections to various foreign policy measures of the government.

The party founded in 1905 upon the Marxian principles of the Rheims-Dresden Resolution attempted to reconcile internationalism and patriotism. The French socialists never once voted for the budget; they never participated in bourgeois ministries, and with the exception of the elections of 1914, they never collaborated with bourgeois parties; they denounced capitalist imperialism and exploitation in Morocco; and they sought "to unify all countries by the collective action of the proletariat." At the same time, the socialists equated the defense of the peace with the defense of national independence. Patriotism for them was an essential ingredient of *inter-nationalism*, the idea that the nation-state complements rather than negates true internationalism. But French socialist patriotism, which implied a love for a common culture, language, and history, was distinguished from "professional patriotism," which the socialists often denounced as fanatical nationalism or chauvinism.[2] If this marriage of class struggle and Jacobin patriotism sometimes resulted in an ambiguous or contradictory foreign policy, as in their attitudes toward French colonial possessions, the socialist concept of national independence preserved in a world of peace by international cooperation was a worthy ideal that has gradually gained acceptance only after two wasteful and tragic wars. Though the socialists erroneously assumed that the aggressor could be easily identified in case of war, their vote for war credits in August 1914 was essentially a reaffirmation of this ideal.

Since the writing of history was begun, historians have usually concentrated on wars, revolutions, and great periods of social, political, and economic upheaval. Those rare periods of peace, which often appear as only dull and gloryless interludes between wars, have invited far less investigation. Similarly neglected have been many of the countless peace groups that have struggled ineffectually for an unarmed world. The French socialists before the First World War are one of those groups; for they believed peace to be a positive accomplishment, not merely a negative interlude between wars. If the study of the past has any value for the present, any lessons to teach or any guidance to offer to a still bewildered and uncertain mankind, it may be profitable to reappraise the program and aspirations of these great idealists.

NOTES

CHAPTER I

1 Milorad M. Drachkovitch, *Les Socialismes français et allemand et le problème de la guerre, 1870-1914* (Geneva: Librairie E. Droz, 1953).

2 Harold R. Weinstein has provided the best treatment of the impact of
Jaurès's patriotic ideas upon the party in *Jean Jaurès, A Study of Patriotism
in the French Socialist Movement* (New York: Columbia University Press,
1936). Marcelle Auclair's *Vie de Jean Jaurès: ou La France d'avant 1914*
(Paris: Editions du Seuil, 1954) and Harvey Goldberg's *Life of Jean Jaurès*
(Madison: University of Wisconsin Press, 1962) are the most complete
accounts of Jaurès's political activities. Goldberg's volume, especially, is the
most well-written and heavily documented biography of Jaurès yet published
and constitutes a key work in the literature of the pre-1914 socialist movement. Among the biographies by Jaurès's contemporaries, Alexandre Zévaès's
Jean Jaurès (Paris: La Clé d'Or, 1951) and Vincent Auriol's *Jean Jaurès*

(Paris: Presses Universitaires de France, 1962) furnish valuable personal recollections, and Charles Rappoport's *Jean Jaurès: L'Homme, le penseur, le socialiste* (Paris: L'Emancipatrice, 1915) continues to rank as the best analysis of Jaurès's ideas.

3 For more detailed studies concerning the emergence of these parties, consult Daniel Ligou, *Histoire du socialisme en France, 1871-1961* (Paris: Presses Universitaires de France, 1962), pp. 23-97, and Georges Lefranc, *Le Mouvement socialiste sous la troisième République, 1875-1940* (Paris: Payot, 1963), pp. 32-95. Aaron Noland's *Founding of the French Socialist Party, 1893-1905* (Cambridge, Mass.: Harvard University Press, 1956) provides valuable background information and traces the development of the party from the legislative elections of 1893 to unification in 1905.

4 Noland, *Founding of French Socialist Party*, 32. This group included 20 Independents, 6 Guesdists, 5 Allemanists, 4 Blanquists, and 2 Possibilists. Alexandre Zévaès's *Histoire du socialisme et du communisme en France de 1871 à 1947* (Paris: Editions France-Empire, 1947), p. 148, gives the figure of 49, but he includes a number of Radical-Socialists and former Boulangists who ran on socialist platforms.

5 For a more thorough explanation of the Saint-Mandé Program, see Noland, *Founding of French Socialist Party*, 48-51.

6 Ligou's *Histoire du socialisme en France*, 140-66, and Noland's *Founding of French Socialist Party*, 86-114, treat the problem of "ministerialism" arising out of the Dreyfus Affair. Rudolph A. Winnacker analyzes the function of Combes's left block in "The Delegation des Gauches: A Successful Attempt at Managing a Parliamentary Majority," *Journal of Modern History*, IX (December 1937), 449-70, and Emile Combes appraises the role of the socialists in his government in *Mon ministère: Mémoires, 1902-1905* (Paris: Librairie Plon, 1956), pp. 97-148.

7 Ligou, *Histoire du socialisme en France*, 166-74. See also Noland, *Founding of French Socialist Party*, 175-84. Auclair treats the role of Jaurès in bringing the unity negotiations to a successful conclusion in his *Vie de Jaurès*, 460-75, and Alexandre Zévaès analyzes the internal structure of the united party in *Le Parti socialiste de 1904 à 1923* (Paris: Librairie des Sciences Politiques et Sociales, 1923), pp. 98-139. The minutes of the Congress of Unity are recorded in *Parti socialiste, section française de l'internationale ouvrière, 1er Congrès national (Congrès d'unité), tenu à Paris les 23, 24, et 25 avril 1905* (Paris: n.d.), pp. 1-43.

8 Paul Louis, *Histoire du socialisme en France de la révolution à nos jours, 1789-1936* (Paris: Librairie des Sciences Politiques, 1936), p. 317. For a discussion of the reasons for the primacy of domestic policy in the Chamber of Deputies among all political parties, especially the Radical-Socialists, see Bertha R. Leaman, "The Influence of Domestic Policy on Foreign Affairs in France, 1898-1905," *Journal of Modern History*, XIV (December 1942), 449-79.

9 The ideas in this paragraph are from Drachkovitch, *Socialismes français et allemand*, 32-34.

10 *Ibid.*, 64.

11 *Ibid.*, 65.
12 *Ibid.*, 66.
13 *Ibid.*, 65.
14 *Ibid.*, 65-66.
15 Zévaès, *Parti socialiste*, 48.
16 Drachkovitch, *Socialismes français et allemand*, 68.
17 *Ibid.*, 67-68.
18 Ligou, *Histoire du socialisme en France*, 93.
19 Drachkovitch, *Socialismes français et allemand*, 68-69.
20 *Ibid.*
21 *Ibid.*
22 *Ibid.* See also Weinstein, *Jean Jaurès*, 27-38.
23 Drachkovitch, *Socialismes français et allemand*, 69-70.
24 *Ibid.*
25 *Ibid.*, 72.
26 *Ibid.*
27 *Ibid.*, 73. Charles-Robert Ageron, in "Jaurès et les Socialistes français devant la question algérienne," *Le Mouvement social*, XLII (January-March 1963), 3-29, states that Jaurès traveled to Algeria in 1895 and returned to France with great sympathy for the Moslem world and a deep conviction that France could implement in Algeria a policy of assimilation and "moral conquest." See also Jean Bruhat's "Jean Jaurès devant le problème colonial," *Cahiers internationaux*, XCIV (March 1958), 46-62.
28 Brynjolf J. Hovde, "The French Socialists and the Triple Entente, 1893-1914," *Journal of Political Economy*, XXXIV (August 1926), 458-78.
29 Drachkovitch, *Socialismes français et allemand*, 74.
30 *Ibid.*
31 Eugene N. Anderson, *The First Moroccan Crisis, 1904-1906* (Chicago: University of Chicago Press, 1930), p. vii.

CHAPTER II

1 *Journal officiel de la République française, Débats parlementaires, Chambre des Députés*, December 8, 1905, pp. 3821-23. Cited hereafter *JO, Chambre des Députés*.
2 *Ibid.*, January 13, 1911, 37-44.
3 This information was obtained from René Samuel (ed.), *Les Parlementaires français, 1900-1914* (Paris: G. Roustan, 1914) and Jean Jolly, *Dictionnaire des parlementaires français* (Paris: Presses Universitaires de France, 1960).
4 *JO, Chambre des Députés*, December 1, 1905, 2664-75.
5 *Ibid.*, December 8, 1905, 3821-23.
6 *Ibid.*, March 6, 1906, 1141-43.
7 *Ibid.*, June 26, 1908, 1386-89.
8 *Ibid.*, November 26, 1908, 2670-73.
9 *Ibid.*, May 17, 1909, 1069.
10 *Ibid.*, October 27, 1910, 2595.

11 *Humanité*, August 29, 1912.
12 *Ibid.*, October 29, November 4, 1907.
13 *JO, Chambre des Députés*, October 25, 1907, 1939.
14 *Ibid.*, March 1, 1906, 1111-14.
15 *Ibid.*, November 29, 1907, 2619-22.
16 *Ibid.*, December 21, 1908, 2971-77.
17 *Ibid.*, December 22, 1908, 2989.
18 Drachkovitch, *Socialismes français et allemand*, 88-89.
19 Weinstein, *Jean Jaurès*, 108.
20 *Humanité*, December 24, 1907.
21 *Ibid.*, December 28, 1907.
22 *Ibid.*, February 14, 1908.
23 *JO, Chambre des Députés*, March 30, 1908, 802-6.
24 Weinstein, *Jean Jaurès*, 107.
25 *Ibid.*, 103. Pages 89-105 of Weinstein's work provide an excellent discussion of the relations between the syndicalists and the socialists during this period. Edouard Dolléans's *Histoire du mouvement ouvrier, 1871-1936* (Paris: Librairie Armand Colin, 1948) is the best treatment of syndicalist attitudes before 1914 toward war and peace.
26 *Humanité*, September 15, 1911; May 26, 1913.
27 Drachkovitch, *Socialismes français et allemand*, 91.
28 *Humanité*, November 3, 1907.
29 *Ibid.*, October 22, 1907.
30 *Parti socialiste, 3ᵉ Congrès national, tenu à Limoges les 1ᵉʳ, 2, 3, et 4 novembre 1906* (Paris: n.d.), pp. 214-64; *Parti socialiste, 4ᵉ Congrès national, tenu à Nancy les 11, 12, 13, et 14 août 1907* (Paris: n.d.), pp. 169-321.
31 *Humanité*, October 4, December 28, 1907.
32 *Journal des débats*, October 11, 1907.
33 See, for example, Lavino's reports in the London *Times* of January 8, 24, and 30, 1908.
34 Charles Péguy, *Oeuvres Complètes*, Vol. 4 (Paris: Editions de la Nouvelle Française, 1916), pp. 182-83.
35 *3ᵉ Congrès national, tenu à Limoges*, 239-45.
36 Hovde, "French Socialists and the Triple Entente," 463.
37 *3ᵉ Congrès national, tenu à Limoges*, 260-64.
38 *4ᵉ Congrès national, tenu à Nancy*, 178-81.
39 *Ibid.*, 315-21.
40 James Joll, *The Second International, 1889-1914* (New York: Praeger, 1956), pp. 133-43, gives the full text of the Stuttgart resolution. See also Patricia van der Esch, *La Deuxième Internationale, 1889-1923* (Paris: Librairie Marcel Rivière et Cie, 1957), pp. 84-96.
41 *Parti socialiste, 5ᵉ Congrès national, tenu à Toulouse les 15, 16, 17, et 18 octobre 1908* (Paris: n.d.), p. 109.
42 *Parti socialiste, 7ᵉ Congrès national, tenu à Paris les 15 et 16 juillet 1910* (Paris: n.d.), pp. 55-71.

43 Joll, *Second International*, 140-43; Esch, *Deuxième Internationale*, 89-95. Consult also Auclair, *Vie de Jaurès*, 262-63; Louis, *Histoire du socialisme en France*, 334-35. For further reports on the Copenhagen congress, see *Humanité*, September 2, 3, 4, 1910.

44 These federations included such areas as the Yonne, Bouches-du-Rhône, Vaucluse, Seine-et-Oise, Creuse, and Basses-Pyrénées. See Ligou, *Histoire du socialisme en France*, 80-84. These, along with the Basses-Alpes, Alpes-Maritimes, Charente-Inférieure, Jura, Somme, and Algeria, joined in support of Hervé's motion on insurrection at the 1906 congress at Limoges.

45 *7ᵉ Congrès national, tenu à Paris*, 70-71.

46 *Parti socialiste, 11ᵉ Congrès national, tenu à Amiens les 25, 26, 27, et 28 janvier 1914* (Paris: n.d.), pp. 77-216.

47 *5ᵉ Congrès national, tenu à Toulouse*, 83.

48 *JO, Chambre des Députés*, February 22, 1906, 470-77.

49 *Ibid.*, March 7, 1906, 1251-57.

50 *Ibid.*, March 15, 1906, 1331-40.

51 *Ibid.*, November 22, 1906, 2647.

52 *Ibid.*, November 23, 1906, 2678-79.

53 *Ibid.*, 2679-81.

54 *Ibid.*, June 7, 1907, 1221-29.

55 *Ibid.*, 1229-32.

56 *Ibid.*, 1234.

57 *4ᵉ Congrès national, tenu à Nancy*, 44.

58 *JO, Chambre des Députés*, November 18, 1909, 2762-71.

59 *Ibid.*, January 16, 1911, 89-91.

60 *Ibid.*, February 23, 1911, 641-55.

61 *Ibid.*, February 26, 1911, 696.

62 *Ibid.*, March 23, 1911, 1730-33.

63 *Parti socialiste, 10ᵉ Congrès national, tenu à Brest les 23, 24, et 25 mars 1913* (Paris: n.d.), pp. 238-62.

64 *JO, Chambre des Députés*, March 26, 1914, 2280-84.

65 *Ibid.*, November 26, 1908, 2663-73.

66 *Ibid.*, December 27, 1909, 3783-92.

67 *Ibid.*, January 18, 1909, 33-46.

68 *Ibid.*, November 18, 1909, 2762-71. Jaurès set forth these same ideas in the Chamber in January 1911. *Ibid.*, January 13, 1911, 33-46.

69 See, for example, the speeches in *JO, Chambre des Députés*, December 14, 1911, 3363-64; December 15, 1911, 3392-97; December 16, 1911, 3442-47; December 19, 1911, 3511-18; December 20, 1911, 3546-51.

70 *10ᵉ Congrès national, tenu à Brest*, 238-62.

71 Louis, *Histoire du socialisme en France*, 341.

72 *Humanité*, March 1 through June 30, 1913.

73 *Ibid.*, August 30, 1910.

74 *Ibid.*, September 1, 1908.

75 *Ibid.*, July 12, 1908; September 22, 1910. See also Jaurès's speech to the Chamber in December 1905 in which he eulogized Bebel and the German

socialists for "standing up to the imperial rulers of Germany." *JO, Chambre des Députés*, December 8, 1905, 3821-23.

76 *Humanité*, March 31, 1912.
77 Zévaès, *Jean Jaurès*, 229-32.
78 *Humanité*, March 4, 1913.
79 *JO, Chambre des Députés*, June 17, 1913, 836-47.
80 *Humanité*, November 25, 26, 27, 1912.
81 Ministère des Affaires Etrangères, *Documents diplomatiques français, 1911-1914*, 3ᵉ série, Vol. VI (Paris: Imprimerie Nationale, 1933), pp. 610-14. A good description of the Inter-parliamentary Conference of Berne is given here by Leon Beau, the French minister in Berne (May 13, 1913).
82 *11ᵉ Congrès national, tenu à Amiens*, 76-77.
83 Louis, *Histoire du socialisme en France*, 335.
84 *Humanité*, July 15, 16, 17, 1914. This is the only source for the congress, since the war interrupted the printing of the minutes of each session.
85 Joll, *Second International*, 157.
86 See, for example, the speeches in *JO, Chambre des Députés* by Jean Bouhey-Allex, March 1, 1906, 1111-14; by Alexandre Varenne, November 29, 1907, 2619-22; by Jaurès, December 21, 1908, 2971-77; by Edouard Vaillant, February 10, 1910, 934; by Albert Thomas, March 23, 1911, 1734-35.
87 *Ibid.*, October 25, 1907, 1939.
88 *Ibid.*, June 13, 1910, 2114-15.
89 Jean Jaurès, *L'Armée nouvelle* (Paris: Publications Jules Rouff, 1911), p. 266.
90 As quoted in Joll, *Second International*, 111. For a more detailed explanation of Jaurès's new army, see Auclair, *Vie de Jaurès*, 265-69; Goldberg, *Life of Jaurès*, 385-89; Drachkovitch, *Socialismes français et allemand*, 135-38; Joll, *Second International*, 110-12. Joll, especially, is critical of Jaurès's military schemes, noting the inappropriateness of his recommendations to pre-1914 military conditions and quoting the SPD intellectual Max Schippel, who commented on *L'Armée nouvelle* that "you can't put a cannon in the bed of every former gunner and give each old sea dog a little warship to put in his farmyard trough or wash tub."
91 *JO, Chambre des Députés*, November 14, 1910, 2794.
92 Louis Lévy, *Anthologie de Jean Jaurès* (Paris: Calmann-Lévy, 1946), p. xxi.
93 *JO, Chambre des Députés*, December 9, 1912, 2931-40.
94 *Ibid.*, March 3, 1913, 802.
95 *Ibid.*, March 6, 1913, 863.
96 See especially the articles in *Humanité* by Marcel Sembat, March 6, 7, 1913; by Jaurès, March 3, 4, 8, 10, 22, 23, 25-27, April 3, 1913; by Thomas, March 11, 13, 1913.
97 *Ibid.*, March 2, 1913.
98 *Ibid.*, March 8, 1913.
99 *Ibid.*, March 19, July 7, 1913.
100 *10ᵉ Congrès national, tenu à Brest*, 238-313.
101 See *Humanité*, March 27-31, 1913, for announcements of planned demonstrations.

102 *Ibid.,* May 26, 1913.

103 See the speeches in *JO, Chambre des Députés* by Jaurès, December 14, 1911, 3363-64; by Vaillant, December 15, 1911, 3392-97; by Sembat, December 16, 1911, 3442-47.

104 Joseph Caillaux, *Mes mémoires,* Vol. III: *Clairvoyance et force d'âme dans les épreuves, 1912-1930* (Paris: Librairie Plon, 1943), p. 103. See also Charles Paix-Séailles, *Jaurès et Caillaux: Notes et souvenirs* (Paris: Eugene Figuière, 1920), p. 134.

105 Caillaux, *Mémoires,* III, 61.

106 *JO, Chambre des Députés,* June 3, 1913, 448-71.

107 *Ibid.,* June 16, 1913, 768-79.

108 *Ibid.,* 781-85.

109 *Ibid.,* 785-91.

110 *Ibid.,* June 17, 1913, 816-29.

111 *Ibid.,* 836-47.

112 *Ibid.,* June 18, 1913, 853-61.

113 *Ibid.,* June 20, 1913, 939-47.

114 See, for example, the proposals of the socialist deputies Etienne Rognon (Rhône), *ibid.,* June 20, 1913, 947-53, and Raoul Briquet (Pas-de-Calais), *ibid.,* June 23, 1913, 987-1003.

115 *Ibid.,* June 26, 1913, 1405-15. The socialists had made the same charge three months earlier in *Humanité,* March 27, 1913.

116 *JO, Chambre des Députés,* July 4, 1913, 1604-6.

117 *Ibid.,* July 9, 1913, 1757-59.

118 *Ibid.,* July 19, 1913, 2208-13.

119 Goldberg, *Life of Jaurès,* 444-45.

120 *11ᵉ Congrès national, tenu à Amiens,* 76-77.

121 For comment on the impact in France of a potential Caillaux-Jaurès coalition, see François Goguel, *Géographie des élections françaises de 1870 à 1951* (Paris: Editions du Seuil, 1951), p. 40.

122 Caillaux, *Mémoires,* III, 153. See also Paix-Séailles, *Jaurès et Caillaux,* 140.

123 Goldberg, *Life of Jaurès,* 454-55.

CHAPTER III

1 Drachkovitch, *Socialismes français et allemand,* 101-4.

2 Hovde, "French Socialists and the Triple Entente," 463.

3 *Ibid.,* 462.

4 *Ibid.,* 463-64.

5 *Ibid.,* 463.

6 As quoted in Georges Michon, *The Franco-Russian Alliance, 1891-1917,* trans. Norman Thomas (London: George Allen and Unwin, 1929), p. 123.

7 Goldberg, *Life of Jaurès,* 347.

8 As quoted in Goldberg, 347.

9 Michon, *Franco-Russian Alliance,* 130.

10 *Ibid.*
11 *JO, Chambre des Députés,* November 10, 1904, 2367-72.
12 *Ibid.,* April 19, 1905, 1539-50.
13 *Ibid.,* May 15, 1905, 1693-95.
14 Auclair, *Vie de Jaurès,* 480-88. See also Drachkovitch, *Socialismes français et allemand,* 124.
15 Hovde, "French Socialists and the Triple Entente," 459.
16 Auclair, *Vie de Jaurès,* 482. E. J. Dillon, noted correspondent for the London *Daily Telegraph,* has claimed credit for inventing the term that stuck, "Bloody Sunday." See his work, *The Eclipse of Russia* (New York: George H. Doran Company, 1918), p. 157.
17 Drachkovitch, *Socialismes français et allemand,* 124.
18 *JO, Chambre des Députés,* January 24, 1905.
19 See the London *Times,* January 30, 1905.
20 *Parti socialiste, 2ᵉ Congrès national, tenu à Chalon-sur-Saône les 29, 30, 31 octobre et 1ᵉʳ novembre 1905* (Paris: n.d.), pp. 74-75.
21 These events are treated more fully in Michael T. Florinsky, *The End of the Russian Empire* (New Haven, Conn.: Yale University Press, 1931), Ch. I; Bernard Pares, *The Fall of the Russian Monarchy* (London: Jonathan Cape, 1939), pp. 76-110; J. L. H. Keep, *The Rise of Social Democracy in Russia* (Oxford: Clarendon Press, 1963), pp. 216-303.
22 Pares, *Fall of the Russian Monarchy,* 93. Count Serge Witte, the czar's president of the Council of Ministers from 1905 to 1906, affirmed that this loan "saved Russia." See his work, *Memoirs of Count Witte,* trans. Abraham Yarmolinsky (Garden City and New Jersey: Doubleday, Page and Company, 1921), p. 308.
23 *JO, Chambre des Députés,* April 12, 1906, 1737-38.
24 *Ibid.,* February 7, 1907, 322-32.
25 *Ibid.,* February 8, 1907, 335-41.
26 *Ibid.,* 341-46.
27 *Documents diplomatiques français,* 2ᵉ série, X (February 13, 1907), 646-47.
28 *Humanité,* October 6, 1907.
29 *Ibid.,* December 31, 1907; January 14, 21, December 26, 1908; January 7, 26, March 6, 1909.
30 *Ibid.,* November 16, 1907.
31 *Ibid.,* November 1, 1907.
32 *Ibid.,* November 21, 1907. See also the articles by Jean Longuet, *ibid.,* December 1, 7, 1907.
33 *Ibid.,* December 7, 1907.
34 *JO, Chambre des Députés,* June 29, 1908, 1412-16.
35 *Humanité,* June 15, 1908.
36 *JO, Chambre des Députés,* June 29, 1908, 1412-16.
37 *Humanité,* June 30, 1908.
38 *Ibid.,* July 1, 1908.
39 *Ibid.*
40 *Ibid.,* July 4, 1908.
41 *JO, Chambre des Députés,* July 8, 1908.

42   See the articles in *Humanité* against the Franco-Russian Alliance and loans to the czar by Sembat, July 9, August 14, 16, 1908; by Longuet, July 17, 1908; by Allemane, July 20, 1908; by Jaurès, November 22, 1908.

43   *5° Congrès national, tenu à Toulouse,* 109.

44   *JO, Chambre des Députés,* November 10, 1904, 2367-72, 2373-88.

45   *Ibid.,* November 3, 1904, 2252-68.

46   *Ibid.,* November 7, 1904, 2305-20.

47   *Ibid.,* November 10, 1904, 2367-72.

48   *Ibid.,* 2372-88.

49   *Ibid.,* November 26, 1908, 2663-73; December 27, 1909, 3783-92; January 18, 1909, 33-46.

50   *Ibid.,* November 26, 1908, 2674-75.

51   *Ibid.,* January 13, 1911, 37-44.

52   See Jaurès's editorials in *Humanité,* October 6, 8, 11, 1908; statement of the party's motion at the 1908 congress at Toulouse denouncing the Austrian action, *5° Congrès national, tenu à Toulouse,* 109. See also Jaurès's speech to the Chamber in January 1911 on the Russian role in the annexation of Bosnia and Herzegovina. *JO, Chambre des Députés,* January 13, 1911, 33-46.

53   *JO, Chambre des Députés,* December 27, 1909, 3782-83.

54   *Ibid.,* January 12, 1911, 19-24.

55   *Ibid.,* January 13, 1911, 37-44.

56   *Ibid.,* December 16, 1911, 3442-47.

57   *Ibid.,* July 7, 1914, 2280-82.

58   Georges Tétard, *Essais sur Jean Jaurès* (Colombes: Centre d'Apprentissage d'Imprimerie, 1959), p. 133.

CHAPTER IV

1   Jacques Chastenet gives a concise summary of the policies of Delcassé in *Histoire de la troisième République,* Vol. III: *La République triomphante, 1893-1906* (Paris: Librairie Hachette, 1955), pp. 253-75. Consult also C. W. Porter, *The Career of Thèophile Delcassé* (Philadelphia: University of Pennsylvania Press, 1936). See the *Journal des débats,* April 15, 1904, for the complete text of the agreement. Paul Cambon's *Correspondance: 1870-1924* (Paris: Editions Bernard Grasset, 1940), pp. 89-98, 125-33, provides a glimpse at the diplomatic origins of the accord. Keith Eubank's *Paul Cambon: Master Diplomatist* (Norman: University of Oklahoma Press, 1960), pp. 61-125, also furnishes a detailed account of its origins and functioning.

2   London *Times,* November 3, 1904. See also Chastenet, *République triomphante,* 272.

3   *JO, Chambre des Députés,* November 10, 1904, 2367-72, 2373-88. Jaurès's speech of November 10 provoked reaction in Berlin. Prinet, the French chargé d'affaires in Berlin, reported to Delcassé that the socialist leader's remarks, which included criticism of the "narrow, egoistic" aims of German diplomacy, had been reviled by many German newspapers, especially

the *Norddeutsche Zeitung*. See *Documents diplomatiques français*, 2ᵉ série, V (November 20, 1904), 547-48. For a fuller discussion of German reaction to the Anglo-French agreement, consult Anderson, *First Moroccan Crisis*, 135-58, 181-95.

4   *JO, Chambre des Députés*, November 12, 1904, 2413-31.

5   Auclair, *Vie de Jaurès*, 489-95.

6   *Journal des débats*, November 18, 1904.

7   Anderson, *First Moroccan Crisis*, 181-95.

8   *JO, Chambre des Députés*, April 7, 1905, 1251-52.

9   Bülow had stated on April 9, 1904, that the Anglo-French accord was a step toward world peace, and on April 12 he told the Reichstag that the agreement was the beginning of a new era of peace. See *Documents diplomatiques français*, 2ᵉ série, V (April 9, 1904), 1-2 (n.).

10   *JO, Chambre des Députés*, April 19, 1905, 1539-45, 1548-59.

11   Goldberg, *Life of Jaurès*, 347-48.

12   Chastenet, *République triomphante*, 286.

13   *JO, Chambre des Députés*, July 11, 1905, 2825-26.

14   *Ibid.*, December 16, 1905, 4034-36.

15   *Ibid.*, February 23, 1906, 987-93.

16   Georges Bonnefous, *Histoire politique de la troisième République*, Vol. 1: *L'Avant-guerre (1906-1914)* (Paris: Presses Universitaires de France, 1956), p. 16.

17   Anderson, *First Moroccan Crisis*, 397-405.

18   *JO, Chambre des Députés*, April 12, 1906, 1735-39.

19   *Ibid.*, November 29, 1906, 2771-72.

20   *Ibid.*, December 6, 1906, 2952-57.

21   London *Times*, April 21, 1905. See also *Journal des débats*, April 21, 1905.

22   The *Groupe Colonial* in parliament, composed of ninety-one members, included men like Delcassé, who became minister of marine in Caillaux's cabinet in 1911, Eugène Etienne, deputy for Algeria, who served as minister of war in the Rouvier ministry (1905-6) and in the Barthou ministry (1913), Gaston Thomson, minister of marine during Clemenceau's ministry (1906-9), François de Maby, deputy for Réunion, who had served as minister of marine and colonies in 1887 and 1888, and Marcel Saint-Germain, senator for Algeria and president of the *Groupe Colonial*. The vice-president of the group was Charles d'Aunay, senator for Nièvre, and the secretary was Auguste Gervais, senator for the Seine. See Samuel, *Parlementaires français*, appendix. Raymond F. Betts points out in his work, *Assimilation and Association in French Colonial Theory* (New York: Columbia University Press, 1961), pp. 4-7, that the *Groupe Colonial* enjoyed great influence within parliament, drawing its strength primarily from the Center parties. Its members, he notes, who adhered to colonial expansion more from local and personal rather than party interest, were primarily former colonial administrators, former military personnel, and deputies from coastal regions. By 1905 there were no less than thirty-five colonial societies in France, the largest being the *Ecole Coloniale* and the *Comité de l'Afrique Français*, to which Generals Lyautey and Gallieni belonged. Bertha R. Leaman, in

Notes for Chapter IV, pages 61-68

"Influence of Domestic Policy," 479, concludes that the impetus for the French colonial drive was provided, not by the Radicals or Radical-Socialists, who took little interest in foreign policy, but by this colonial group that exercised an influence on foreign policy far out of proportion to its size.

23 Jacques Chastenet, *Histoire de la troisième République*, Vol. IV: *Jours inquiets, jours sanglants, 1906-1919* (Paris: Librairie Hachette, 1957), p. 46.
24 *Journal des débats*, March 29, 1907.
25 *JO, Chambre des Députés*, March 26, 1907, 824-32.
26 The socialists singled out nine of the largest French commercial and industrial enterprises in Morocco in *Humanité*, December 13, 1907, noting the low wages and wretched working conditions under which the Moroccan natives suffered.
27 Ima Christian Barlow, *The Agadir Crisis* (Chapel Hill: University of North Carolina Press, 1940), pp. 48-52.
28 *4ᵉ Congrès national, tenu à Nancy*, 577; *Humanité*, October 6, 1907.
29 See the daily articles in *Humanité* throughout October, November, and December, 1907, and throughout the first six months of 1908. Consult especially the editorials of December 29, 1907, and January 15, 25, 26, March 1, 2, May 29, 31, and August 28-31, 1908.
30 See *JO, Chambre des Députés*, October 22, 1907, 1895; November 12, 1907, 2153-57; November 13, 1907, 2194-95; November 28, 1907, 2572-73; December 5, 1907, 2807-8; January 24, 1908, 95-108; January 27, 1908, 115-47; February 10, 1908, 267-70; February 24, 1908, 413-27; March 27, 1908, 769-86; June 19, 1908, 1276-87; July 7, 1908, 1590-92.
31 *Documents diplomatiques français*, 2ᵉ série, XI (January 29, 1908), 260-61.
32 *Ibid.*
33 *Humanité*, August 28, 1908.
34 *Ibid.*, September 1, 1908.
35 *5ᵉ Congrès national, tenu à Toulouse*, 55-65.
36 *Humanité*, November 7, 1908.
37 *Documents diplomatiques français*, 2ᵉ série, XI (May 22, 1909), 1075-80.
38 Barlow, *Agadir Crisis*, 68.
39 *Ibid.*, 76-77.
40 *Humanité*, February 11, 1909.
41 *Ibid.*, February 10, 1909.
42 *JO, Chambre des Députés*, November 22, 1909, 2823-28; November 23, 1909, 2831-40; February 18, 1910, 927-30; March 25, 1910, 1659-70.
43 Barlow, *Agadir Crisis*, 207.
44 *Ibid.*, 170.
45 *JO, Chambre des Députés*, March 14, 1911, 1481-83.
46 *Ibid.*, March 24, 1911, 1796-1811.
47 *Ibid.*, June 16, 1911, 2321-32.
48 Barlow, *Agadir Crisis*, 207-37.
49 *Ibid.*
50 *Humanité*, July 2, 1911.
51 *Ibid.*, July 3, 1911.
52 *JO, Chambre des Députés*, July 4, 1911, 2547.

53 *Ibid.*, July 11, 1911, 2738-39.
54 *Humanité*, July 13, 1911.
55 See the articles in *Humanité* by Sembat, July 14, August 2, 1911; by Thomas, July 30, 1911; by Allard, August 11, 1911.
56 *Ibid.*, September 15, 1911.
57 *Ibid.*, September 21, 1911.
58 *Ibid.*, September 25, 1911.
59 *Ibid.*, September 26, 1911.
60 *Ibid.*, October 25, November 1, 10, 1911.
61 *JO, Chambre des Députés*, December 12, 1911, 3251-55.
62 *Ibid.*, December 14, 1911, 3363-64; December 15, 1911, 3392-97; December 16, 1911, 3442-47; December 19, 1911, 3511-18; December 20, 1911, 3546-51.
63 *Ibid.*, December 15, 1911, 3397.
64 *Ibid.*, December 20, 1911, 3564-65.
65 These included Guesde himself, Compère-Morel, Hubert Rouger, Charles Dumas, Raoul Briquet, Pierre Myrens, Gustave Delory, Jean Colly, Gäetan Albert-Poulain, Arthur Groussier, Paul Mistral, Gustave Dubled, Pierre Brizon, and Léon Betoulle.
66 *JO, Chambre des Députés*, March 8, 1912, 809-29.
67 *Ibid.*, March 15, 1912, 1137-44.
68 *Ibid.*, January 19, 1912, 42-46. For further comment on the Tunisian scandal, see Goldberg, *Life of Jaurès*, 546-47.
69 *JO, Chambre des Députés*, February 1, 1912, 201.
70 *Ibid.*, February 2, 1912, 226.
71 *10ᵉ Congrès national, tenu à Brest*, 286-313.
72 *JO, Chambre des Députés*, February 29, 1912, 662.
73 *Ibid.*, June 28, 1912, 1912-26.
74 *Ibid.*, July 1, 1912, 1955-65.
75 See Abel Ferry, *Les Carnets secrets d'Abel Ferry (1914-1918)* (Paris: Grasset, 1958), *passim*.
76 Joseph Paul-Boncour, *Souvenirs sur la IIIᵉ République*, Vol. 1: *Entre deux guerres, 1877-1918* (New York: Brentano's, Inc., 1946), p. 224.

CHAPTER V

1 Alexandre Zévaès, *La Question d'Alsace-Lorraine et le socialisme* (Paris: Editions du Comité de Propagande Française Républicaine et Réformiste, 1917), pp. 58-59.
2 Ligou, *Histoire du socialisme en France*, 208.
3 See Zévaès, *Jean Jaurès*, 151.
4 *Ibid.*, 213.
5 *Ibid.*
6 *JO, Chambre des Députés*, November 10, 1904, 2373-88.
7 *Documents diplomatiques français*, 2ᵉ série, VII (November 11, 1904), 545-46.
8 *JO, Chambre des Députés*, November 26, 1908, 2670-73.

9 *Ibid.*, January 18, 1909, 33-46.
10 *Ibid.*, November 18, 1909, 2762-71.
11 *Humanité*, May 26, 1911.
12 See Lévy, *Anthologie de Jaurès*, 94.
13 *Humanité*, August 22, 1912.
14 *10ᵉ Congrès national, tenu à Brest*, 238-62.
15 *JO, Chambre des Députés*, April 7, 1908, 905-13.
16 *Humanité*, June 30, 1908.
17 For further comment on the Bosnia crisis of 1908, see Bernadotte E. Schmitt, *The Annexation of Bosnia 1908-1909* (Cambridge, England: Cambridge University Press, 1937).
18 *Humanité*, October 11, 1908.
19 *Ibid.*, October 8, 1908.
20 *Ibid.*, October 6, 1908.
21 *Ibid.*, October 13, 1908.
22 *Ibid.*, October 14, 1908.
23 *5ᵉ Congrès national, tenu à Toulouse*, 109.
24 *JO, Chambre des Députés*, January 15, 1909, 23-26.
25 *Humanité*, February 26, 1909.
26 *Ibid.*, January 1, February 26, 27, 28, March 29, 1909.
27 *Ibid.*, February 28, March 14, 1909.
28 *Parti socialiste, 6ᵉ Congrès national, tenu à Saint-Etienne les 11, 12, 13, et 14 avril 1909* (Paris: n.d.), pp. 404-5.
29 *JO, Chambre des Députés*, December 27, 1909, 3783-92.
30 *Humanité*, April 10, 1909.
31 *Ibid.*, September 3, 1910.
32 *JO, Chambre des Députés*, November 26, 1908, 2673-75.
33 *Humanité*, October 6, 1908.
34 *Ibid.*, July 15, August 30, October 6, 1908.
35 *Ibid.*, September 19, 1911.
36 *Ibid.*, September 30, 1911.
37 *Ibid.*, October 1, 1911.
38 *Ibid.*, September 15, 1911.
39 *Ibid.*
40 *Parti socialiste, 9ᵉ Congrès national, tenu à Lyon le 18, 19, 20, et 21 février 1912* (Paris: n.d.), pp. 97-99.
41 *Ibid.*
42 *Humanité*, November 4, 1911.
43 *Ibid.*, October 26, 1912.
44 Weinstein, *Jean Jaurès*, 151.
45 *Humanité*, August 30, 1908.
46 *JO, Chambre des Députés*, January 15, 1909, 23-26.
47 *Ibid.*, November 26, 1908, 2673-75.
48 *Ibid.*, January 13, 1911, 37-44.
49 Ernest Christian Helmreich, *The Diplomacy of the Balkan Wars* (Cambridge, Mass.: Harvard University Press, 1938), pp. 101-45, 192-230.
50 *Humanité*, October 2, 1912.

51 *JO, Chambre des Députés*, January 13, 1911, 37-44.
52 *Humanité*, October 2, 3, 7, 8, 1912.
53 *Ibid.*, October 10, 14, 20, November 10, December 10, 12, 13, 1912.
54 *Ibid.*, October 7, 14, 1912.
55 *Ibid.*, October 9, 11, 13, 15, 16, 18, 20, 21, 26, November 13, 15, 18, 23, 26, December 16, 23, 1912.
56 *Ibid.*, October 18, 1912.
57 *Ibid.*, October 29, 30, 1912.
58 *Ibid.*, November 18, 1912.
59 *Ibid.*, November 29, 1912.
60 For reports on the congress at Basel, see *Humanité*, November 25, 26, 27, 28, 1912. See also Joll, *Second International*, 153-57; Esch, *Deuxième Internationale*, 105-12.
61 *JO, Chambre des Députés*, December 21, 1912, 3346-48.
62 *Ibid.*, June 16, 1913, 781-91.
63 *Humanité*, June 24, July 1, 1913.

CHAPTER VI

1 See Eugene Weber, *The Nationalist Revival in France, 1905-1914* (Berkeley and Los Angeles: University of California Press, 1959), p. 138; William Curt Buthman, *The Rise of Integral Nationalism in France* (New York: Columbia University Press, 1939), pp. 516-17; Goldberg, *Life of Jaurès*, 452-53. For a geographical analysis of the election, see Goguel, *Géographie des élections*, 64; Lefranc, *Mouvement socialiste*, 427; Ligou, *Histoire du socialisme en France*, 231. Those departments where the SFIO made its largest gains included Haute-Vienne, Allier, Nord, Ardennes, Nièvre, Var, Bouches-du-Rhône, Cher, Pas-de-Calais, Isère, Gard, Aube, Yonne, Rhône, Saône-et-Loire, Hérault, Aude, Haute-Garonne, and Tarn.
2 *Humanité*, June 29, 1914.
3 *Ibid.*
4 *JO, Chambre des Députés*, July 7, 1914, 2280-82.
5 For the reports on this congress, see *Humanité*, July 15, 16, 17, 1914.
6 *Ibid.*, July 17, 1914. See also Goldberg's account of the debates at the 1914 congress at Paris in his *Life of Jaurès*, 460-62.
7 *Humanité*, July 25, 1914.
8 Louis, *Histoire du socialisme en France*, 343-44.
9 *Humanité*, July 28, 1914.
10 *Ibid.*
11 *Ibid.*, July 29, 1914.
12 *Ibid.* See also Louis, *Histoire du socialisme en France*, 344.
13 Goldberg, *Life of Jaurès*, 466-67.
14 *Humanité*, July 31, 1914.
15 Marcel Prélot, *L'Evolution politique du socialisme français, 1789-1934* (Paris: Editions Spés, 1939), p. 203.
16 *Humanité*, July 30, 1914.

17 Louis, *Histoire du socialisme en France*, 344-45.
18 Goldberg, *Life of Jaurès*, 469.
19 *Humanitè*, July 31, 1914.
20 Prélot, *Evolution politique*, 203.
21 Tétard, *Essais sur Jaurès*, 133.
22 Louis, *Histoire du socialisme en France*, 346.
23 *Ibid.*, 5.
24 *Humanité*, August 3, 1914.
25 *Ibid.*
26 Louis, *Histoire du socialisme en France*, 348.
27 *JO, Chambre des Députés*, August 4, 1914, 2312-15.
28 William H. Maehl, "The Triumph of Nationalism in the German Socialist Party on the Eve of the First World War," *Journal of Modern History*, XXIV (March 1952), pp. 15-41.

CHAPTER VII

1 Goldberg, *Life of Jaurès*, 341.
2 Weinstein, *Jean Jaurès*, 4-5.

BIBLIOGRAPHY

1 GOVERNMENT DOCUMENTS

Journal officiel de la République française, Débats parlementaires, Chambre des Députés. October 1904-August 1914. The verbatim report of the proceedings of the Chamber of Deputies.

Ministère des Affaires Etrangères. *Documents diplomatiques français, 1871-1914.* 2ᵉ série, Vols. V-XI; 3ᵉ série, Vols. I-XI. Paris: Imprimerie Nationale, 1929-38, 1948-55.

2 PARTY RECORDS

Parti socialiste, section française de l'internationale ouvrière, 1ᵉʳ Congrès national (Congrès d'unité), tenu à Paris les 23, 24, et 25 avril 1905. Paris, n.d.

Parti socialiste . . . 2ᵉ Congrès national, tenu à Chalon-sur-Saône les 29, 30, 31 octobre et 1ᵉʳ novembre 1905. Paris, n.d.

Parti socialiste . . . 3ᵉ Congrès national, tenu à Limoges les 1ᵉʳ, 2, 3, et 4 novembre 1906. Paris, n.d.

Parti socialiste . . . 4ᵉ Congrès national, tenu à Nancy les 11, 12, 13, et 14 août 1907. Paris, n.d.

Parti socialiste . . . 5ᵉ Congrès national, tenu à Toulouse les 15, 16, 17, et 18 octobre 1908. Paris, n.d.

Parti socialiste . . . 6ᵉ Congrès national, tenu à Saint-Étienne les 11, 12, 13, et 14 avril 1909. Paris, n.d.

Parti socialiste . . . 7ᵉ Congrès national, tenu à Nîmes les 6, 7, 8, et 9 février 1910. Paris, n.d.

Parti socialiste . . . 7ᵉ Congrès national, 2ᵉ session, tenu à Paris les 15 et 16 juillet 1910. Paris, n.d.

Parti socialiste . . . 8ᵉ Congrès national, tenu à Saint-Quentin les 16, 17, 18, et 19 avril 1911. Paris, n.d.

Parti socialiste . . . 9ᵉ Congrès national, tenu à Lyon les 18, 19, 20, et 21 février 1912. Paris, n.d.

Parti socialiste . . . 10ᵉ Congrès national, tenu à Brest les 23, 24, et 25 mars 1913. Paris, n.d.

Parti socialiste . . . 11ᵉ Congrès national, tenu à Amiens les 25, 26, 27, et 28 janvier 1914. Paris, n.d.

3 PERIODICALS AND NEWSPAPERS

Humanité. October 1904-August 1914. The largest and most influential socialist newspaper during this period, edited by Jaurès and published at Paris.

Journal des débats. April 1904-August 1914. A conservative weekly magazine published at Paris.

London *Times.* October 1904-August 1914. The daily reports of Philip Lavino, Paris correspondent.

4 MEMOIRS AND PUBLISHED LETTERS

Bompard, Maurice. *Mon ambassade en Russie, 1903-1908.* Paris: Librairie Plon, 1937.

Caillaux, Joseph. *Mes mémoires.* Vol. III: *Clairvoyance et force d'âme dans les épreuves, 1912-1930.* Paris: Librairie Plon, 1943.

Cambon, Paul. *Correspondance, 1870-1924.* Paris: Editions Bernard Grasset, 1940.

Combes, Emile. *Mon ministère: Mémoires, 1902-1905.* Paris: Librairie Plon, 1956.

Paul-Boncour, Joseph. *Souvenirs sur la IIIe République.* Vol. 1: *Entre deux guerres, 1877-1918.* New York: Brentano's, Inc., 1946.

5 BOOKS AND ARTICLES

Ageron, Charles-Robert. "Jaurès et les Socialistes français devant la question algérienne." *Le Mouvement social,* XLII (January-March 1963), 3-29.

Anderson, Eugene N. *The First Moroccan Crisis, 1904-1906.* Chicago: University of Chicago Press, 1930.

Auclair, Marcelle. *La Vie de Jean Jaurès: ou La France d'avant 1914.* Paris: Editions du Seuil, 1954.

Auriol, Vincent. *Jean Jaurès.* Paris: Presses Universitaires de France, 1962.

Barlow, Ima Christian. *The Agadir Crisis.* Chapel Hill: University of North Carolina Press, 1940.

Betts, Raymond F. *Assimilation and Association in French Colonial Theory.* New York: Columbia University Press, 1961.

Boitel, Maurice. *Les Idées libérales dans le socialisme de Jean Jaurès.* Paris: Université de Paris (Faculté de droit), 1921.

Bonnefous, Georges. *Histoire politique de la troisième République.* Vol. 1: *L'Avant-guerre (1906-1914).* Paris: Presses Universitaires de France, 1956.

Brogan, Denis W. *The Development of Modern France (1870-1939).* London: Hamish Hamilton, 1940.

Bruhat, Jean. "Jaurès et les Guerres coloniales." *Europe*, XXXVI (October-November 1958), 74-81.

———— "Jean Jaurès devant le problème colonial." *Cahiers internationaux*, XCIV (March 1958), 43-62.

Buthman, William Curt. *The Rise of Integral Nationalism in France*. New York: Columbia University Press, 1939.

Carrol, E. Malcolm. *French Public Opinion and Foreign Affairs, 1870-1914*. New York: Columbia University Press, 1931.

Challaye, Félicien. *Jaurès*. Paris: Melotteé, 1937.

Challener, Richard D. *The French Theory of the Nation in Arms, 1866-1939*. New York: Columbia University Press, 1955.

Chastenet, Jacques. *Histoire de la troisième République*. Vol. III: *La République triomphante, 1893-1906*; Vol. IV: *Jours inquiets, jours sanglants, 1906-1919*. Paris: Librairie Hachette, 1955, 1957.

Clarke, Jack Alden. "French Socialist Congresses, 1876-1914." *Journal of Modern History*, XXXI (December 1959), 124-29.

Cole, G. D. H. *A History of Socialist Thought*. Vol. III, Parts I and II: *The Second International, 1889-1914*. London: Macmillan and Company, 1956.

Compère-Morel, Adéodat, *Jules Guesde, le socialisme fait homme, 1845-1922*. Paris: A. Quillet, 1937.

Derruau-Boniol, Simone. "Le Socialisme dans l'Allier de 1848 à 1914." *Cahiers d'histoire*, II (March 1957), 115-62.

Dillon, E. J. *The Eclipse of Russia*. New York: George H. Doran Company, 1918.

Dolléans, Edouard. *Histoire du mouvement ouvrier, 1871-1936*. Paris: Librairie Armand Colin, 1948.

Dommanget, Maurice. *Edouard Vaillant, un grand socialiste, 1840-1951*. Paris: La Table Ronde, 1956.

Drachkovitch, Milorad M. *De Karl Marx à Leon Blum*. Geneva: Librairie E. Droz, 1955.

——— *Les Socialismes français et allemand et le problème de la guerre, 1870-1914.* Geneva: Librairie E. Droz, 1953.

Esch, Patricia van der. *La Deuxième Internationale, 1889-1923.* Paris: Librairie Marcel Rivière et Cie, 1957.

Eubank, Keith. *Paul Cambon: Master Diplomatist.* Norman: University of Oklahoma Press, 1960.

Ferry, Abel. *Les Carnets secrets d'Abel Ferry (1914-1918).* Paris: Grasset, 1958.

Figuères, Léo. "Jaurès et l'Armée nouvelle." *Europe,* XXXVI (October-November 1958), 81-86.

Florinsky, Michael T. *The End of the Russian Empire.* New Haven, Conn.: Yale University Press, 1931.

Frossard, L. O. *Sous le signe de Jaurès: Souvenirs d'un militant.* Paris: Flammarion, 1943.

Garaudy, Roger. *Jaurès et la paix.* Paris: Editions Sociales, 1949.

Garber, Elizabeth. "L'Arbitrage international devant le mouvement socialiste français, 1890-1914." *Revue socialiste,* CV (February 1957), 293-313.

Garnier-Thenon, Michael. "Jaurès et l'Armée nouvelle." *Revue socialiste,* CXLVIII (January 1961), 504-20.

Girault, René. "Sur quelques aspects de l'alliance Franco-Russe." *Revue d'histoire moderne et contemporaine,* VIII (October 1961), 67-76.

Goguel, François. *Géographie des élections françaises de 1870 à 1951.* Paris: Editions du Seuil, 1951.

Goldberg, Harvey. *The Life of Jean Jaurès.* Madison: University of Wisconsin Press, 1962.

Gouttenaire de Toury, F. *Jaurès et le parti de la guerre.* Paris: Rieder, 1922.

Guy-Grand, Georges. "Jaurès, ou Le Conciliateur." *La Grande Revue,* VII (July 1918), 3-20.

Halévy, Elie. *Histoire du socialisme européen.* Paris: Librairie Gallimard, 1948.

Helmreich, Ernest Christian. *The Diplomacy of the Balkan Wars.* Cambridge, Mass.: Harvard University Press, 1938.

Hovde, Brynjolf J. "The French Socialists and the Triple Entente, 1893-1914." *Journal of Political Economy*, XXXIV (August 1926), 458-78.

Jaurès, Jean. *L'Armée nouvelle.* Paris: Publications Jules Rouff, 1911.

Joll, James. *The Second International, 1889-1914.* New York: Praeger, 1956.

Jolly, Jean. *Dictionnaire des parlementaires français.* Paris: Presses Universitaires de France, 1960.

Keep, J. L. H. *The Rise of Social Democracy in Russia.* Oxford: Clarendon Press, 1963.

Larguier, Léo. *Le Citoyen Jaurès.* Paris: Portiques, 1932.

Leaman, Bertha R. "The Influence of Domestic Policy on Foreign Affairs in France, 1898-1905." *Journal of Modern History*, XIV (December 1942), 449-79.

Lefranc, Georges. *Le Mouvement socialiste sous la troisième République, 1875-1940.* Paris: Payot, 1963.

Lévy, Louis. *Anthologie de Jean Jaurès.* Paris: Calmann-Lévy, 1946.

Ligou, Daniel. *Histoire du socialisme en France, 1871-1961.* Paris: Presses Universitaires de France, 1962.

Louis, Paul. *Histoire du socialisme en France de la révolution à nos jours, 1789-1936.* Paris: Librairie des Sciences Politiques, 1936.

Maehl, William H. "The Triumph of Nationalism in the German Socialist Party on the Eve of the First World War." *Journal of Modern History*, XXIV (March 1952), 15-41.

Marmande, R. de. "French Public Opinion and the Russo-Japanese War." *Fortnightly Review*, LXXXII (September 1904), 317-23.

Michon, Georges. *The Franco-Russian Alliance, 1891-1917*. Trans. Norman Thomas. London: George Allen and Unwin, 1929.

Noland, Aaron. *The Founding of the French Socialist Party, 1893-1905*. Cambridge, Mass.: Harvard University Press, 1956.

Paix-Séailles, Charles. *Jaurès et Caillaux: Notes et souvenirs*. Paris: Eugene Figuière, 1920.

Pares, Bernard. *The Fall of the Russian Monarchy*. London: Jonathan Cape, 1939.

Péguy, Charles. *Oeuvres Complètes*. Vol. 4. Paris: Editions de la Nouvelle Française, 1916.

Porter, C. W. *The Career of Thèophile Delcassé*. Philadelphia: University of Pennsylvania Press, 1936.

Prélot, Marcel. *L'Evolution politique du socialisme français, 1789-1934*. Paris: Editions Spés, 1939.

Pressensé, Francis de. "England, France, Germany, the Peace of the World." *Contemporary Review*, LXXXVIII (June 1905), 153-62.

———— "France, Morocco, and Europe." *Contemporary Review*, XCII (January 1907), 731-39.

Rappoport, Charles. *Jean Jaurès: L'Homme, le penseur, le socialiste*. Paris: L'Emancipatrice, 1915.

Rosmer, Alfred. *Le Mouvement ouvrier pendant la guerre*. Paris: Librairie du Travail, 1936.

Samuel, René (ed.). *Les Parlementaires français, 1900-1914*. Paris: G. Roustan, 1914.

Schmitt, Bernadotte E. *The Annexation of Bosnia 1908-1909*. Cambridge, England: Cambridge University Press, 1937.

Tétard, Georges. *Essais sur Jean Jaurès*. Colombes: Centre d'Apprentissage d'Imprimerie, 1959.

Thomas, Raymond. "La Politique socialiste et le Problème colonial de 1905 à 1920." *Revue française d'histoire d'outre-mer*, LVIII (February 1960), 213-45.

Valiani, Léo. *Histoire du socialisme au XXe siècle*. Paris: Les Editions Nagel, 1948.

Weber, Eugene. *The Nationalist Revival in France, 1905-1914*. Berkeley and Los Angeles: University of California Press, 1959.

Weinstein, Harold R. *Jean Jaurès, A Study of Patriotism in the French Socialist Movement*. New York: Columbia University Press, 1936.

Winnacker, Rudolph A. "The Delegation des Gauches: A Successful Attempt at Managing a Parliamentary Majority." *Journal of Modern History*, IX (December 1937), 449-70.

Witte, Count Serge. *Memoirs of Count Witte*. Trans. Abraham Yarmolinsky. Garden City and New Jersey: Doubleday, Page and Company, 1921.

Zévaès, Alexandre. *Histoire du socialisme et du communisme en France de 1871 à 1947*. Paris: Editions France-Empire, 1947.

———— *Jean Jaurès*. Paris: La Clé d'Or, 1951.

———— *Le Parti socialiste de 1904 à 1923*. Paris: Librairie des Sciences Politiques et Sociales, 1923.

———— *La Question d'Alsace-Lorraine et le socialisme*. Paris: Editions du Comité de Propagande Française Républicaine et Réformiste, 1917.

INDEX

128

131